WAVE RIDER

Also by Harrison Owen

Open Space Technology

Spirit: Transformation and Development in Organizations

Leadership Is

Riding the Tiger

The Millennium Organization

Tales From Open Space

Expanding Our Now: The Story of Open Space Technology

The Power of Spirit: How Organizations Transform

The Spirit of Leadership

WAVE RIDER

Leadership for High Performance in a Self-Organizing World

HARRISON OWEN

BK

Berrett–Koehler Publishers, Inc.
San Francisco
a BK Business book

Berrett-Koehler Publishers, Inc.

235 Montgomery Street, Suite 650

San Francisco, CA 94104–2916

Tel: (415) 288–0260 Fax: (415) 362–2512 www.bkconnection.com

ORDERING INFORMATION

Quantity sales. Special discounts are available on quantity purchases by corporations, associations, and others. For details, contact the "Special Sales Department" at the Berrett-Koehler address above.

Individual sales. Berrett-Koehler publications are available through most bookstores. They can also be ordered directly from Berrett-Koehler:
Tel: (800) 929–2929; Fax: (802) 864–7626; www.bkconnection.com

Orders for college textbook/course adoption use. Please contact Berrett-Koehler:
Tel: (800) 929–2929; Fax: (802) 864–7626.

Orders by U.S. trade bookstores and wholesalers. Please contact Ingram Publisher Services, Tel: (800) 509–4887; Fax: (800) 838–1149; E-mail: customer.service@ingrampublisherservices.com; or visit www.ingrampublisherservices.com/Ordering for details about electronic ordering.

Berrett-Koehler and the BK logo are registered trademarks of Berrett-Koehler Publishers, Inc.

Printed in the United States of America

Berrett-Koehler books are printed on long–lasting acid–free paper. When it is available, we choose paper that has been manufactured by environmentally responsible processes. These may include using trees grown in sustainable forests, incorporating recycled paper, minimizing chlorine in bleaching, or recycling the energy produced at the paper mill.

Library of Congress Cataloging–in–Publication Data

Owen, Harrison, 1935–
Wave rider : leadership for high performance in a self-organizing world / Harrison Owen.
p. cm.
ISBN 978-1-57675-617-1 (pbk. : alk. paper)
1. Leadership. 2. Management. I. Title.

HD57.7.O9425 2008
658.4'092—dc22
2008025598

Book Producer: Tolman Creek Media
Book Editor: Pat Brewer

To All The Wonderful People Who Helped Me On This Journey

Contents

Preface

W ith this book I have come to the end of a cycle of thinking and writing which began some 40 years ago. By way of introduction I would like to share some-thing of that history.

An unpublished dissertation, written in 1965, could have had the subtitle, "Chaos, Order, and the Creative Process." As a matter of fact the dissertation dealt with arcane approaches to biblical inter-pretation, particularly as this related to the nature and function of myth. But through the esoterica of biblical scholarship there appeared a continuing theme: the great cosmic dance of chaos and order. I have been working that theme ever since.

As it turned out, my life path, and the world of biblical schol-arship radically diverged at roughly the time I wrote that disserta-tion, thanks to the Civil Rights movement. Suddenly I found myself living the dance of chaos and order as opposed to merely reading and thinking about it.

The next several years were full to the point of bursting. Street organizing in the South, running a large poverty program in Washington, DC, off to Africa with Peace Corps as Associate Director in Monrovia, Liberia, back to the United States to head up a health care infrastructure development program. Then on to the National Institutes of Health to create the professional, public, and

Peter suggested that I write an article bearing the title ,
"Mythology and Organizational Culture." I sent the piece off to a
prestigious journal (Peter told me which one) to await instantaneous
acclamation. Shortly thereafter I received a response, but not exactly
the one I was hoping for. The editor said that the whole thing was
so far out that it lacked credibility and could not be published. That
was 1979 and the notion that organizations had cultures and myths
was rather beyond what the market would allow.

I guess I should have learned better, but I was hooked, if for no
other reason than that two disparate strands of my life (academic
and activist) came together with a rush, taking me to places that
few others seemed interested in going. From the myth, ritual, and
culture in organizations I found myself venturing deeper into what
the stories were saying, and it wasn't what most of my peers and
colleagues seemed to think was being said.

According to the contemporary wisdom, organizations were
engaged in a linear developmental process which some did exceedingly well, and others less so. For the latter there was a lot of help
available, all under the heading of Organization Development.

My read was rather different. I could see the developmental
process, but I also thought I could see virtually instantaneous, radical state change. And the odd thing was, these organizations actually
seemed to be going somewhere useful, but their trajectory was anything but the standard, linear model. There was only one word that
described it for me: transformation. And the fundamental mechanism was none other than the great dance of chaos and order.

It was but a small step, as I saw it, to join the words "transformation" with "organization" to create Organization Transformation.

As it turned out several friends had been having similar thoughts and we became what some people referred to as "The OT Cabal." The focal questions were simple: What does transformation in organizations look like, and what, if anything, could we do about it?

We met in odd places for long and intense conversations—the favorite was The Penguin, a nondescript restaurant in Rosalyn, Virginia. The usual guest list included John Adams, Linda Ackerman, Frank Burns, Jim Channon, Lisa Kimball—and of course Peter Vaill. Somewhere along the line I presented a paper (with my friend David Belle Isle) at a regional Organization Development Network (ODN) conference with the title, "Myth and Ritual as the Ground of Organization Transformation." I have lost that paper, but I recall the concluding lines. "I don't really have a clue what Organization Transformation is, but I think it may well be the natural successor to Organization Development, suitable for life, and work in a transforming world."

The reaction to this paper was intense, and startlingly so to me. So far as I was concerned we had only put two words together (organization and transformation) to mark out an interesting area for study, and perhaps practice. Others perceived it in rather different terms as a confrontation between OD and OT. It was also very clear that the conversation circle was expanding, and needed to expand even more if we were to have any hope of really understanding what we were talking about.

Expansion came with the convening of the 1st International Symposium on Organization Transformation which took place in Durham, New Hampshire in the summer of 1983. Two hundred and fifty people joined the original OT Cabal. We began with the clear recognition that we were starting from ground zero when it came to definition and understanding. By the conclusion I think it is fair to say that we were still wandering about in the wilderness, but now at least there were a lot more colleagues.

One of the spin-offs from this first symposium was Open Space Technology (OST). It didn't happen immediately, but it became clear to me that although it had all been great fun and very stimulating, the truly juicy parts took place at the coffee breaks. This was a shock because we had spent basically a year organizing everything, and yet the truly delicious stuff took place only in the parts we didn't organize.

Two years later (1985) I agreed to convene the same gathering one more time, but resolved never to go through again the extended agony of preparation. Open Space Technology seemed like the right thing to do—and we did. As some of you know, OST is simplicity itself. Sit in a circle, create a bulletin board, open a marketplace, and go to work. One facilitator, no interventions, and everything runs all by itself. The resulting conversations were rich and the journey toward understanding Organization Transformation seemed well on its way.

My own effort in this area showed up as my first book, *Spirit: Transformation and Development in Organizations* (Abbott Publishing). I could say that I wrote the book, but it would be much more accurate to say that the book wrote me. Truthfully I had no idea what the next chapter would be until I started to write it. And guess what? It was all about chaos, order, and the creative (transformative) process, with side trips into the worlds of myth, ritual, and the evolution of human consciousness.

I wrote that book for myself, just to see if there was any logic
and coherence in the jumble of thoughts and feelings of the preceding years. However, when I shared it with friends they urged me
to do something more with it, and so the typescript pages found
their way between two covers, and became a book. *Spirit*, as it came
to be known, was never a contender for the best-seller list, but it
did seem to have a useful life which continues online. Its one real
point of notoriety came when the *Utne Reader* called it a "cult classic."
I am sure they were sincere, and I never really understood what
they were talking about, but what I did understand made me a
little nervous.

More books came tumbling out during the 1990s—*Riding the
Tiger, The Millennium Organization, Leadership Is* (all published by
Abbott Publishing). Some of my friends chided me gently for what
they saw to be repetitiousness, and I had to confess that I was
guilty as charged. But what are you going to do when there is a
single, overriding theme in all of your work—Chaos, Order, and the
Creative Process? Besides, I came to recognize that I was much
more of a storyteller than an academic author, and a major characteristic of storytellers is that they tell the same tale over and over,
each time turning it slightly to reveal a different facet.

This was also the time frame when chaos and complexity theory
came into the public view, and although most of the proponents
were physicists, chemists, and biologists I came to look at them as
colleagues on a common journey. On the rare occasions when we
actually met, I did feel constrained to point out that their "New
Science" was indeed exciting, but perhaps not all that new. As near
as I could tell, serious thinking about chaos and order had been

ongoing for probably three or four thousand years, back to the days
of the Babylonian Creation Epic with the tales of Marduk and Tiamat.

In 1992 I published *Open Space Technology: A User's Guide*, some
seven years after the first Open Space. My reasons for writing the
book were quite practical. As Open Space spread, and more and
more people used it—even more people wanted to know how to
do it. A book seemed a reasonable solution.

At the same time my own perceptions of OST were changing
quite radically. Initially OST was only a simple way to solve a
bothersome problem; organizing conferences. OST clearly accomplished that objective. However, a new problem was created.
Virtually all of the theory and practice relating to organizing meetings, to say nothing of organization in general, indicated that OST
could not work. But it did. How come?

Whatever the reason, it was apparent that OST played by some
very different rules, and the only rules that seemed to apply were
those we were all learning from the world of self-organizing systems. Even more curious was the apparent fact that much of what I
had been thinking and writing about under the heading of
Organization Transformation appeared to be taking place in OST
gatherings. Without intention, obvious effort, or preparation—
meeting in Open Space appeared to be transformative.

I can't say that this new appreciation of Open Space occurred
in a blinding flash, but there came a point when I realized that I
had serendipitously been placed in the midst of an ongoing natural
experiment. We had a clearly articulated process (experimental procedure) which was now being run all over the world by multiple
people in wildly differing situations.

As the experiment progressed, some very definite and interesting results turned up. Two in particular caught my attention. First was elevated levels of performance, sometimes remarkably so. Groups did in a few days what they might normally expect to accomplish in months. The second I could call only the appearance of peace. Not the sort of peace where everybody fell asleep, or sat around chanting *ommn*, but a very active and dynamic sort of peace in which conflicting forces coalesced and danced with each other. It would have been wonderful to see all of this as the direct result of my creation, Open Space Technology, but something of a deeper sort was taking place. The critical element was not OST— but rather the force of self-organization, which I now understood to be the driving power of OST.

If any of that was true, it would make sense to eliminate the middle man (OST) and go straight to the source. The operating hypothesis might be, *Well-functioning self-organizing systems are naturally productive of peace and superior performance.* Briefly stated, the eternal dance of chaos and order is the fundamental process of self-organization. When that dance is done well, positive and surprising things will happen (High Performance and Peace). And when the dance falters the emergent organization will struggle or die.

I made several efforts to pull all of this together, not only as a theoretical package, but more importantly, as a practical application. In two books (*The Power of Spirit* and *Expanding Our Now*, Berrett-Koehler) I detailed my observations and thoughts. It worked for me, but nobody seemed to be very impressed. In retrospect I can see that there was too much theory and a lack of focus on practical application. In self-defense I might cite Kurt Lewin who said, "There is nothing so practical as a good theory," but that really did not change the situation. Practical focus was essential, and current events provided the needed impetus.

On September 11th, 2001 the world changed radically. Old perceptions and answers simply evaporated, leaving massive questions. What was happening and what could we do about it? In the midst of all of this I was invited to the Middle East. I found myself, quite literally, in the belly of the beast with hardly a clue as to why I was there, or what I could do. On the night before our program I was sitting on the rooftop of an Israeli friend near Tel Aviv. The night was soft and gentle with a full moon and little puffball clouds moving slowly by. The tranquility of the night contrasted sharply with my discordant feelings, only adding to my confusion. Then suddenly, almost as a dream I found myself speaking to that night—"It's all about the Practice of Peace."

The Practice of Peace became the title of my most recent book, published by the Human Systems Dynamics Institute. I proposed that when Peace is threatened, the appropriate response is simply to open space. In doing so the chaotic, conflicted human systems are invited to do what only they can do–self-organize to new and higher levels of complexity more in harmony with each other, their environment, and their own inner needs. Practically this could mean "doing an Open Space," but could also mean utilizing the fundamental learnings from the 20 year Open Space Experiment.

The impetus for this present book was not of the same world shattering sort which occasioned *The Practice of Peace*, but the two books are definitely related. It occurred that a Finnish group asked that I come to their country and share what I have been learning and doing. I suggested something along the lines of *The Practice of Peace* as a starting point. This suggestion was greeted with a long period of silence, at the end of which my Finnish colleagues said that while they personally were very concerned about peace, most of their clients were corporate. They were not at all sure that a program on peacemaking would receive official sanction (financial support) from the several training departments. And did I have any other thoughts?

By happenstance I had just re-read Peter Vaill's seminal paper, "The Behavioral Characteristics of High Performing Systems," and I noticed something I had never seen before. Vaill's behavioral characteristics described to perfection the performance of groups operating in Open Space. Could it be, I wondered, that the root source of these behaviors was nothing other than the power of self-organization? If so, high performance might be achieved through the simple expedient of opening space and inviting the system to fully self-organize. The thought seemed reasonable to me, and never being one to worry about the details, I said to my Finnish colleague that in fact I did have another thought. If they did not like Peace, how about High Performance?

One problem solved, but another immediately presented itself. What was I going to say? After reflection it occurred to me that the logic and structure of the "Peace" book would work quite well for another effort dealing with High Performance. Of course, the focus and examples would be very different, but the basic thought that a fully functional self-organizing system was (by definition) a high performing system was the same. In fact it seemed to me that a peaceful system, and a high performing system were one and the same, it just depended on how you looked at them.

Here, if never before, I could justifiably be accused of repetition, a simple change in words, but no change in substance. Guilty as charged, but in my defense I would point out that as a storyteller I have only performed as storytellers throughout the ages have performed. In revisiting my lifelong central theme of chaos, order, and the creative process, I have turned the theme once again to reveal a different facet. Whether that turn, and the revealed facet, is worthy of your attention I leave to your judgment as you read this book.

Introduction
Wave Rider

Wave Riders are curious people possessed of an innate capacity to go with the flow, constantly seizing upon opportunity when others see no possibility, or even disaster. Their level of performance is consistently high, and projects are often completed in breathtakingly short periods of time, with a degree of excellence that may seem unbelievable. Not always, not in every instance—but with a regularity that sets them apart, but never alone. Together with their fellows, Wave Riders create the critical community bonds, essential for productive activity. And they bring a special gift—Leadership. Their passion and responsibility for a cause inspire others to make common cause. Not by domination and control, but through invitation and appreciation, the efforts of many coalesce as one.

Saying that Wave Riders go with the flow is not to say that they have a light regard for planning, logic, and hard work. In fact the Wave Rider may be a fanatic for planning, logical to a fault, and a total workaholic. But what sets them apart is that they also possess a clear understanding of the limitations of all three: planning, logic, and hard work. For them the Plan is the map and not the territory. Necessary, useful, but never to be confused with the facts on the ground, and certainly never to be given preeminence.

Likewise with logic. Good and useful for sure, but when the daily course of experience appears to behave in an illogical fashion, usually referred to as counterintuitive, the Wave Rider will understand that there are multiple "logics," and it may well be that the one employed is simply inappropriate to the situation. A classic case of this phenomenon comes from the world of physics at the point where quantum mechanics made its appearance. Traditional Newtonian physicists were logical to a fault, perceiving the elegant coherence in the cosmos to be an exquisite clockworks. However, as the world of subatomic physics became the object of study, the traditional logic faltered. And those who were crafting the emerging quantum physics used the sense of illogic to advance their work. Werner Heisenberg, the originator of the Uncertainty Principle, is said to have remarked, "Your theory is crazy, but not crazy enough to be true."

On the subject of work—Wave Riders do indeed work very hard. They are often sticklers for detail and devote amazing amounts of time and energy to enterprises for which they have a genuine passion. When they care, they care deeply, and the effect of this caring is a devotion to their cause that others may find disturbing.

But there is another aspect to a Wave Rider's relation to work that many will find strange. On occasion, all of their busy *doing* simply stops. The task lists are put away, the goals and objectives are all placed on hold. The Wave Rider is content to be there in that present moment. An outside observer might legitimately conclude that the Wave Rider has given up, but the truth is rather different. She or he has simply let go. Not to be confused with a fatalistic withdrawal from life—this letting go has a very different quality. The commitment to the original passionate concern remains unshaken, and if anything, is deepened and intensified. Rather than fatalism, there is profound awareness and trust in the deep forces which drive toward completion and fulfillment. And of equal importance is a recognition that any "doing" in the sense of organizing, managing, forcing—will not only be ineffective, but may well be counterproductive.

Wave Riders may be found in all times and places. Some will be remembered as major historical characters, the names of others will never be recorded in the pages of history. Gandhi, for example, confounded the British Empire not only with his tireless efforts and articulate strategy (plans), but also, and perhaps more importantly, with his presence and capacity to simply be there in the present moment, apparently doing nothing. Dee Hock comes from a very different environment, the corporate world. As the founder of VISA International, Dee Hock surely *did* a lot, but he also well understood the need to let go and simply be there. Not the controlling/directing chief executive, but rather the appreciator of an evolving organic entity which has become one of the largest global corporations—and over which he had no control.

Wave Riders are not limited to global or corporate heros. The mother of a growing family, shepherding her brood toward adulthood, will ride the waves of her complex and confusing world—multi-tasking we call it. To be sure, she has plans and tasks in abundance, to-do lists without end. But at the end of the day, and indeed on every day, she will be remembered not so much for what she did, which may be truly awesome, but rather for the power of her singular presence.

Wave Riders show up on the shop floor and the executive suite, athletic fields, and the halls of government. They appear at every level and station in life, but never are they to be confused with the great man version of The Leader, even though some may bear the most exalted of titles. The power of their presence comes from a very different place. It is not bestowed as a divine right, nor is it claimed in a decisive act of control. It is a power that comes from powerlessness and the full recognition that they will never be in control. They do not command; they invite. They do not envision themselves at the apex of a hierarchy but rather in a circle with their peers and colleagues. The source of their power comes from their own unique passion linked to responsibility which attracts others to join a common venture. A venture which is at once productive and personally fulfilling for those who care to join. Wave Riders are leaders who enable individuals and organizations to fulfill their potential—with distinction.

Needed: More Wave Riders

Wave Riders have been with us always, usually unnoticed, or if noticed then treated as a curious exception to the rule. And indeed it often seemed that they were playing by very different rules. There was doubtless a time when we could afford to smile sympathetically at the behavior of the Wave Riders in our midst. When good things happened (the difficult was handled with dispatch, and the impossible achieved with a little more time), we could scratch our heads and wonder at the fabulous run of luck which the Wave Rider obviously enjoyed. It would never occur to us that there might actually be a method in their madness. In fact such thoughts *could not* occur to us if only because virtually all of our training and experience told us otherwise. Wave Riders were clearly the exception, and we all knew the proper way to do business, whatever that business might be. The critical point was to seize and maintain control in the manner of the Great Man Leader. Only then could good and useful things happen. Or so many of us thought.

The times have changed. The anomalous behavior of the Wave Rider holds a critical clue to new ways of surviving, and indeed thriving, in our chaotic world, enabling all of us to achieve levels of excellence and high performance previously unknown.

The search for high performance has typically been a major concern of businesses and other organizations in their quest for efficiency and effectiveness. However, the stakes have risen dramatically. Achieving optimum levels of human performance is no longer just an issue of organizational effectiveness, but now a matter of global survival. The list of threatening possibilities is virtually without end: climate change, nuclear disaster, pandemics of various sorts, to name a few. Any one of these, taken by itself, would constitute a real problem, but everything is coming together in a dizzying maelstrom of complex interaction. Even just thinking about all of this is sufficient to produce the maximum headache. The good news is that for the past several millennia, human beings have successfully negotiated the terrain. Not always perfectly, and perhaps less than elegantly, but so far we have made it. However, more than a few disturbing signs indicate that our good luck may be about to change, signs which appear as organizational dysfunction, and individual fatigue and disorientation.

The simple fact of the matter is that our institutions, major and minor, are stretched to the breaking point. Even with the best efforts in the world, the stuff accumulating in the Global Inbox is getting out of hand. The impact on our individual lives is equally obvious and severe. Stress, breakdown, alienation, exhaustion— we know them all. Rather like the mad Queen in Alice and Wonderland, we are discovering that the faster we go, the "behinder" we get.

Doubtless the end is not yet, and for sure we have a few more tricks up our sleeves. However, the time may well have come when the consideration of alternatives would be useful. Typically, we have attempted to deal with our multiple dilemmas by trying harder and harder to do more and more of what we have always done. If our organizations lack purpose and power, it is obviously time to reorganize—and reorganize again. And when events show every indication of spinning into oblivion, we redouble our efforts to assert, or regain, control—layering controllers upon controllers upon controls. I propose that it is not that we are doing something wrong, but rather that we are doing the wrong thing. Or put somewhat differently: Going the way we are going we are not likely to reach our destination. It is time for a change of course.

The argument of the book is that we must now recognize that we, our organizations, as indeed the entire cosmos—are all self-organizing systems. Not just a little bit, not just in some special part, but from beginning to end, top to bottom. It is all self-organization. The implications of this recognition, should it prove to be valid, are twofold (at least). First, a large part of what we currently devote a good deal of time and energy to—organizing things—is wasted effort, for our systems, left to their own devices, will take care of that business pretty much all by themselves. Second, our efforts at organization and control are not only of questionable value, but also destructive. By imposing our view of organization on a self-organizing system we essentially throw a spanner in the works, thereby reducing organizational function and our own levels of performance.

Stated in more positive terms, were we to recognize, and fully appreciate, the power of self-organization we could be relieved of an enormous task, freeing time and energy for the many other pressing issues of our day. Even better, we might learn how to leverage the power of self-organization for our benefit, thereby achieving levels of performance which presently lie beyond our wildest dreams. We will ride this primordial power, compensating for our own powerlessness. Wave Riders for sure.

Secret of the Wave Rider

The Wave Rider's secret is a deep awareness of the fundamental self-organizing nature of our world. This awareness may be largely intuitive or very conscious, but the net effect is the capacity to align oneself and one's work with the primal force of self-organization, thereby leveraging its enormous power. Concurrently, the Wave Rider is keenly aware of the limitations of his or her own powers, particularly the power of control. Recognizing the mind-boggling complexity of the chaordic forces at play (thank you, Dee Hock) the Wave Rider understands that total control, at least of the sort that many seem to seek, is but a fond hope, verging on the delusional.

The image of the Wave Rider comes from the world of surfing, providing a vivid picture of the interrelationship of human beings and the self-organizing world. To see the point, we must set the scene as a surfer might experience it. At the simplest level there is a lot of ocean, more than a few waves, and a very small board—with the beach lying ahead. The objective is quite simple. Ride the wave on the board until you reach the beach. Although there may be many mis-steps, mishaps, and false starts along the way, when The Wave comes it can be the experience of a lifetime.

For somebody sitting on the beach, particularly a non-surfer such as myself, the setting looks like simplicity itself—waves, board, beach, and sky. An experienced surfer will see all this rather differently, beginning with the wave(s).

The elegant simplicity of the forming wave is a monster of complexity with quite a history. For a West Coaster (U.S.) the story begins in the vastness of the Pacific. A gentle wind ruffles an otherwise smooth surface and a wavelet is born. As more and different winds transverse the surface, wavelets coalesce in a complex process of cancellation and amplification. And curiously enough the water itself hardly moves, it is only the force passing through, modified by intervening islands and continents. And so the forming wave has a history which vastly exceeds the time from the first puff of wind. The movement of tectonic plates and violent volcanic events from millennia past also make their mark.

When the wave force swells the waters off the California coast, local powers and conditions add their imprint to the complex stew. Bottom types of differing sorts shift and form the surfacing wave until it rises from the surrounding sea and comes into the view of the waiting surfer. Simple on the surface, but containing a churning mammoth of complex, interacting forces with a very long history.

When the instant arrives that rider, wave, and board unite—all of the history, complexity, skill, surging power, and random chaos coalesce in a mindless moment of sheer exhilaration. Speeding down and across the broad face of the advancing wave with the curl steaming spray just behind and above—the rider, board, and wave are one in a timeless moment. Sooner or later that moment comes to an end, as all things do in this life. But for that moment an image of high performance is accelerated by the leveraged power of an enormous self-organizing system, otherwise known as the Pacific Ocean.

What can we learn from the surfer that may assist us in our own efforts to ride the waves of our time with excellence, manifesting true high performance? The two primary lessons may appear largely negative but no less important. First, if we ever thought that the road forward might be viewed solely as a rational project which we might think our way into, we clearly have a second thought coming. The level of random complexity, to say nothing of chaos, confusion, and conflict is more than sufficient to blow the superior mind. We simply can't think that sort of stuff, and certainly not to the point where we could identify, isolate, analyze, and understand the myriad critical elements.

This does not mean, of course, that good, hardheaded fact gathering, analysis, and "intentioning" (used to be called Planning) are irrelevant. Such efforts have their place, but they need to be kept in their place. All of that is, and remains, a map of the territory, never to be confused with the reality of the wave face and the incredible timeless moment of hanging out there.

The second lesson relates to the subject of control. Stated bluntly, any surfer who ever thinks, even for an instant, that he or she is in charge of the wave, is in for a profound shock, delivered in a most memorable way. Assuming, of course, that there is any memory left to capture the moment.

And yet perfect rides on perfect waves do take place—despite the mind-numbing complexity of the moment, and the ultimate lack of control. It might appear to be dumb luck, but if so, the luck is not randomly distributed. Very clearly, some surfers "really get it" and others do not do so well. Obviously technique and experience play a significant part, but when the ride begins, there is no time to run through the checklist of the 42 critical points for a great ride. Once on the wave face and the descent begins—the rules have definitely changed. In the instant technique and experience are included but also radically transcended.

The metaphor of the Wave Rider, like all metaphors, has its limitations. I am hopeful, however, that it will serve to carry us into the world of self-organizing systems not as helpless pieces of flotsam and jetsam tossed about in a chaotic world, but rather as conscious and sensate human beings capable of bringing the human adventure to interesting and fulfilling conclusions.

The fundamental limitation of the Wave Rider image is that it may take us back into the troubled waters of rampant individualism, and the notion that leadership for high performance is the private preserve of The Great Man. But the solo rider coursing down the face of a giant wave, the Mavericks[1] for example, is but a moment in time. And behind and ahead of this

---

1 The Mavericks are a magnificent set of waves that appear periodically off the coast of California. And when the surf is up surfers from around the world gather for the rides of their lives, with thousands of spectators cheering them on from the beach.

moment lie innumerable rides by countless individuals over time. Surfing is a community activity, and each individual who stands for the moment in splendid isolation on the wave face is supported by the skills and enthusiasm of thousands of colleagues. It is true. One person surfs alone, expressing his passion for the ride and taking full responsibility for the consequences. But it is only a moment, and a shared moment at that. Fellow surfers share the wave face, and others will follow on succeeding waves.

The big secret is that we are all Wave Riders, but some do better than others. As long as human beings have inhabited Planet Earth, we have existed in a self-organizing world. Quite probably the majority are simply unconscious of this fact, and their adjustment to the forces of self-organization are equally unconscious. Others are unwilling Wave Riders, who take deep umbrage at the uncontrollable forces at play, seeking their defeat and claiming to be in charge. This effort may appear successful in the short term, but ultimately the powerful waves of our world pass on by undiminished, leaving those who thought they were in charge looking a little silly. There have also been more than a few who truly understood the situation, if only intuitively, and learned to ride the waves to their benefit and to the benefit of their fellow human beings. We are all Wave Riders, and the purpose of this book is to enable each one of us to become intentionally and competently what we already are—riders on the waves.

Invitation to an Experiment

I recognize that the propositions stated above represent somewhat of a departure from the conventional ways of viewing organizations and our place in them. Therefore I have no hope or expectation that these propositions will be easily or quickly accepted. In fact, doing so would be counterproductive. There is much to think about, rigorously examine, and test before anything approaching proof can be claimed. Therefore, you are invited to join an experiment, which in fact (at least as far as I am concerned) is already under way.

The experiment comes in two phases, the first part began some 21 years ago with the creation of Open Space Technology (OST)[2], which as you may know is credited to my account. I believe that credit to be largely undeserved as I rather stumbled into OST, but telling that story must wait until later in the book.

OST, for those unfamiliar with the approach, is simplicity itself. Groups of people sharing a common concern for a complex issue are invited to sit in a circle, identify the relevant sub-issues by posting them on a bulletin board, work out the time and space arrangements for their discussions in a marketplace setting—and then go to work. There is no prior training, or "warm-up activities," little obvious facilitation, and for all pretenses and purposes, the whole thing runs all by itself. I hasten to add that this is not just another book about Open Space Technology, although it is certainly about *open space*, which in my lexicon describes the special circumstances and conditions necessary for the initiation and sustenance of self-organization.

---

2 See *Open Space Technology: A User's Guide, 3rd* Edition (Owen/Berrett-Koehler, 2008).

The utter simplicity of OST contrasts starkly with the results commonly achieved. Very large groups of people (2000+) are enabled to deal with massive, conflicted, and complex issues in a respectful and productive fashion—all in a very short period of time. From the point of view of conventional meeting and organizational management theory and practice—the demonstrated results simply could not happen. But they do, and continue in thousands of situations around the world. In seeking to understand this phenomenon the only adequate theoretical base that I have discovered is that provided by the work of various disciplines with the process of self-organization.

It is my intention to use the collective experience with OST as the point of departure for the deeper discussion of self-organization, our human systems as self-organizing, and the ways in which we may support and optimize their levels of performance. Ultimately this is about learning (remembering) and exercising our roles as Wave Riders, the true leaders in a self-organizing world. In this context, the 21-year experience with Open Space Technology becomes a natural experiment with all the strengths and limitations of such experiments.

Natural experiments, by definition, are unplanned, and in the case of OST that is definitely the case. The unplanned nature of such experiments means that many, if not all, of the standard controls are simply not in place, rendering confidence in the results open to question—until the sheer number of iterations tend to compensate for the possible effect of odd variables. Open Space Technology has now been run in excess of 100,000 times in 136 countries with comparable results. The experiment continues; however, my personal comfort level with the results to date is such that I believe we are in a position to gather up the lessons learned about life in self-organizing systems and move on to the next phase of the natural experiment. We will use these lessons from OST as a basis for scaling up the enterprise—moving from the rather narrow confines of time/space limited events to the expanded and more critical realm of real, live organizations, large and small.

Preview of Coming Attractions

The book is divided into two parts. Part I, *Preparation for Wave Riding*, details the basic argument of the book (There is no such thing as a non–self-organizing system) and suggests the means and methods which will be of assistance when living and working in our self-organizing world. Part II, *The Wave Rider's Guide to the Future*, converts the more general and theoretical discussion of Part I into a practical approach. If your natural predilection is toward the practical, you may do well to reverse the order. Your choice.

In Part I, we begin with a consideration of the Holy Grail of all Wave Riders, and just about everybody else: Superior performance at the individual and organizational level. Peter Vaill, whose seminal work in this area initiated the contemporary discussion, referred to all of this collectively as a High Performing System (HPS). Curiously, he declined to actually define an HPS, however this omission is understandable since we always seem to recognize such creatures when we meet. Quite simply they do what they do with distinction, and in any event, outperform the competition. What Vaill chose not to define, he could clearly describe, which he did in a short, but nevertheless watershed paper bearing the title, "Towards a Behavioral Description of High Performing Systems"[3]

Rushing in where Vaill chose not to go, I propose a possible definition of High Performance as the absence of its (apparent) opposites: Chaos, Confusion, and Conflict. The suggestion being that if only we could eliminate this troublesome trio, the high performance of our systems would be a surety. Unfortunately it seems that all three (especially the first—Chaos) are essential to life, and thus their elimination would not only fail to usher in high performance, but would usher out life. Which leaves us with the interesting problem of defining (understanding) high performance as including, but somehow transcending, chaos, confusion, and conflict.

My formulation goes as follows:

High Performance is the productive interplay of diverse, complex forces, including chaos, confusion, and conflict, characterized by wholeness, health, and harmony. It is *harmonious,* including all elements of harmony both consonance and dissonance, in that multiple forces work together to create a unitary flow. It is whole in the sense that there is a clear focus, direction, and purpose. It is healthy in that the toxins of its process (metabolic by-products in organisms) are eliminated effectively, and without prejudice to itself or environment. High Performance can never be sustained at the cost of a fouled nest. A *High Performing System* is one that does all of the above with excellence, over time, and certainly better than the competition.

---

3 The paper was originally a photocopied "pass around" for friends and colleagues. Eventually it was published in *Leadership: Where Else Can We Go?* edited by Morgan McCall, Duke University Press, 1978. Vaill eventually did create a definition, which appears in his paper, *Purposing.*

Presuming that this definition, combined with the behavioral characteristics identified by Peter Vaill, is sufficient to indicate the object of our inquiry, the next question is simple: How do we get there from here? How do we bring our systems to the level of high performance?

For many of us the answer has come in terms of what might be called the Problem/Solution approach. When it is perceived that performance levels are declining, this is determined to be a problem for which a "fix" must be found. The simple and obvious logic of the approach has much to commend it, and in truth it is quite effective, at least in the short term. However, over time difficulties arise, usually in terms of unintended consequences. The identified problem is fixed, but a host of new problems are generated which are as bad, or worse, than the original situation.

More recently, it has become apparent that the difficulty with the approach derives from the narrowness of the view. By concentrating on a single problem and searching for a single fix, the larger aspects of the system and its environment are essentially ignored. And this ignorance comes back to bite us.

Enter Systemic Thinking. When searching for enhanced performance, we must consider the whole system, including all of its relations with the surrounding environment. This marvelous idea has enabled us to begin to comprehend the mind-blowing complexity of the human systems of our lives. However, when it comes to the successful conclusion of our search for high performance, the systems approach in its various manifestations (e.g., Business Process Re-Engineering) leaves something to be desired. In fact it might actually be seen as an exercise in futility.

The more precisely we identify the operative elements and relationships in our systems, the more it becomes clear that we confront a level of complexity that has no end. And when it comes to redesigning (re-engineering), the task is daunting. However, a daunting task could turn into a wonderful opportunity if we only had the time to complete our system's analysis before everything changed again. And here the cookie crumbles.

In our restless world, every thing is connected and everything is moving. Even worse, most of that connection and movement lies beneath (beyond) our capacity to apprehend. To add insult to injury, the chaos and complexity theorists tell us that the root of our problem lies with a funny little butterfly flapping its wings in Thailand, thereby changing the weather patterns in California. To date that butterfly remains at large, hidden in an undisclosed location.

We might note that the conventional "Great Man" theory of leadership fits very naturally with the Problem/Solution approach, as well as its latter day reincarnation in Systemic Thinking where the "problem" becomes the whole system, and the fix becomes more complicated. The Great Man will define the problem and then decisively administer the fix, which is precisely why he is known as The Leader. However, to the extent that both approaches struggle or fail, so also does the Great Man theory of leadership.

Given the level of effort and our success to date, a monumental state of depression could well be justified—except for the fact that High Performing Systems continue to show up in our experience, but rarely where we expect them, and definitely not according to The Plan. Ordinary people do extraordinary things, under the most unlikely circumstances. We consider such manifestations as anomalies, funny little exceptions to the rules.

By definition, an *anomaly* is something that happens "outside the law" (Greek *a nomos*, "without law")—outlaws, so to speak. These are the sorts of things that everybody knows could not, or should not happen—but they did. Upon closer examination it usually turns out that the anomaly was no outlaw. Either our perception was flawed, and we failed to see how the law applied or (much more rarely), the anomaly was totally within the law, but it was just a different law than we were used to. The latter situation can be a matter of real discomfort, particularly if we have a major attachment to the old law. But the learning opportunity is profound, for we may be at the edge of discovering a totally new way of looking at our world. According to Thomas Kuhn, this is the moment of Paradigm Shift.

Now for The Open Space Technology Experiment. For more than 20 years, thousands of groups of people have gathered around issues of common concern which manifest such levels of complexity and conflict as to make resolution appear impossible. Following a 15-minute introduction, the group defines its issues, deals with the practicalities of time and place of meeting—and goes to work. There is no prior agenda setting, only a single facilitator who never intervenes in the discussions—and at the end of the day (or more usually two days) the accomplishments are real, and very often quite unbelievable. Perhaps most remarkable, there is not a sign of The Leader, great man or woman. Nobody is in charge.

For example, a $200,000,000 structure was designed, starting with a blank sheet of paper, and ending with working architectural drawings. Actually this was a re–design, occasioned by major changes in plans and circumstances. The previous effort had taken 10 months, and thus the group had managed to do in two days what they knew, on the basis of prior experience, would take 10 months. Figuring roughly, this comes down to a 15,000% increase in productivity, and the executive responsible described the outcome as "magic."

In fact it was not magic, but rather a significant (but not unique) application of Open Space Technology. This is definitely an anomaly within an anomaly. What the people accomplished represents a severe challenge to credibility, and certainly the participants found it incredible ("magic"). But *how* they managed to achieve their results doesn't make any sense at all. Indeed it would seem to violate virtually every principle and procedure of group management and probably management practice as well. Talk about different rules!

If this book were simply about Open Space Technology, the tale might end right here and I could accept whatever accolades, as the originator of OST. In fact I know those accolades would be undeserved, and the tale has only just begun.

Searching for the *how* behind, or beneath, Open Space Technology takes us directly into the emerging science of chaos and complexity, and most particularly into the world of self–organizing systems. Of particular interest is the work of Stuart Kauffman, a biologist from the Santa Fe Institute, who has proposed that given certain very simple preconditions, order happens. The correlation between Kauffmann's preconditions, and what I had described as the essential conditions for the use of OST, is virtually 100%, and so it is a natural step to the conclusion that the operative force beneath OST was none other than the primal power of self–organization.

Should you ask—is this true, my response can only be, I think so. At the very least the identification of OST with self–organization provides the only rational explanation I have encountered for an otherwise completely anomalous occurrence. If OST is not magic, it must be self–organization, or so I propose.

Going forward, the logic is clear and simple. If superior performance (HPS) is the common result of OST, and OST itself is a manifestation of the power of self–organization, it would make sense to remove the "middle man" (OST). Or put somewhat differently, if we were able to initiate and sustain the force of self–organization, it should be possible to achieve high performance on some regular basis. We might call this, *The Care and Feeding of Self–organizing Systems*. At this point we arrive at the core realization of all Wave Riders. Not only do we live in a self–organizing world, but our job—or perhaps better, our opportunity, is to leverage this force for our purposes and so ride the waves of self–organization as an intentional and conscious act.

In developing the material which appears in Part II, *The Wave Rider's Guide to the Future* (Chapter 9 and following), I have kept in mind the interests of a younger friend. I'll call him Steve. After reading the manuscript of this book, Steve said that while he loved all the stuff about self–organizing systems, he still had a business to run, bills to pay, and product to get out the door. And he wasn't at all sure that any, or all, of this could be accomplished through self–organization. He didn't say it, but I think he was asserting that, "Somebody simply has to take charge."

It occurred to me at the time that I should wish him a great deal of luck, but not much encouragement. For after all, if my major premise is correct (There is no such thing as a non–self-organizing system), Steve, and all the other "Steves" in the world really don't have any choice. It's all self–organizing. And the notion of "taking charge," as in *running* that system (his business)— just doesn't quite fit.

That said, I take his point and feel his concern. In fact there are multiple concrete steps Steve can take which will enable (but by no means guarantee) that bills are paid and product leaves the premises. I have outlined these steps, along with a number of examples from my own experience and the experience of colleagues. I would hasten to add that none of the material should be confused with the final version of *The Wave Rider's Guide*. The experiment continues, and the final word has yet to be spoken.

The book concludes with an imaginary tale describing a *Day in the Life of a Wave Rider*, along with a tale from a genuine Wave Rider, Dee Hock of VISA International. *The Day in the Life* is imaginary only in the sense that it is described from the point of view of you the reader; however all the reported events and strategies actually took place in my own experience or the experience of friends and colleagues. Dee Hock and VISA are definitely not imaginary.

PART I

Preparation for Wave Riding

A s with all roles and tasks, Wave Riding requires preparation. It is essential to identify what we are looking for (in this case High Performance), the environment we will be operating in, and some of the basic mechanisms and obstacles to be encountered along the way. In addition, the limitations and shortfalls of previous efforts in the quest for High Performance will be considered to the extent that this is helpful in understanding the unique position of Wave Riders, and the waves upon which they ride.

Chapter I

The Holy Grail: Superior Performance

I n 1975, my friend and colleague Peter Vaill (at that point the Dean of the Business School at George Washington University) wrote a short paper which turned out to be long on influence. The paper bore the academic sounding title, "Towards a Behavioral Description of High Performing Systems," However, as Peter was quick to admit, the academics were only skin deep, if only because he found himself "unable to say what a High Performing System is." So much for academic precision, and it gets worse. It turns out that the thoughts expressed did not result from careful research but rather from "intuitive leaps" most of which occurred in "one four hour burst." In fairness, Vaill carefully identified each of his Behavioral Characteristics as "hypotheses," which indicates that they are subject to future validation, although he says nothing about how such research might be conducted, and expresses no interest in pursuing it. At whatever risk, I can only say—It worked for me.

It is true that many have written about high performance in human systems before and after Peter Vaill, but the appearance of his paper was a watershed in my estimation. Those of us who happened to receive a copy found our view of organizations, the way they were supposed to work, and how we might work with them changed in ways that, at least in my own case, would take years to fully appreciate. Some of the other recipients of the paper obviously came to a quicker (and positive) conclusion, most notably Peters and Waterman. Peter Vaill's "intuitive leaps" became a cornerstone of a much larger effort which hit the streets bearing the title, *In Search of Excellence*.[4]

The fact that many of the organizations cited by Peters and Waterman as being "excellent" have now gone out of business does not detract from the powerful impact of this book. Indeed, it might be said that the history of organization and management thought during the succeeding years has been all about that search for what has turned out to be a most elusive quarry—Excellence. Or, were we to revert to the words of Peter Vaill, High Performing Systems. In short, we have been pursuing excellence and High Performance ever since, but somehow we never quite get there. Or perhaps more accurately, we never quite get there "according to the plan." Excellence and high performance keep showing up—but rarely when we might expect them, even less when we planned on their arrival. But all of that is to get considerably ahead of our story, which properly begins with Peter Vaill's "Behavioral Characteristics."

The Behavioral Characteristics of High Performing Systems according to Peter Vaill

In the 1977 revision of his earlier paper, Vaill identifies some 52 characteristics. With frankness uncharacteristic of most academic papers

---

4 Thomas J. Peters and Robert H. Waterman, *In Search of Excellence: Lessons from America's Best-Run Companies* (HarperCollins, 1982).

he admits to certain favorites. In his own words, "Some hypotheses I am in love with and some I am not very interested in." For the most part, Vaill's favorites are those characteristics that would pertain to systems of all sorts, and the balance is more narrowly focused on businesses, and particularly manufacturing businesses (with machines). Following Vaill's lead, I have focused on the favorites. The numbers at the end of each quote are Vaill's original numbers.

- **Do Not Follow the Rule Book** ("There may be a public, objective theory or 'rule book' about how to do the thing that the HPS is doing, but there will always be discrepancies between this public recipe and what the HPS is actually doing. This may be called the 'Doug Sanders backswing' hypothesis to remind golfer–readers that orthodoxy is not an absolute virtue." #7)

- **Members Can't Explain It** ("Communication about how and why the HPS operates as it does from members to outsiders will tend to be in platitudes and generalities, or by showing rather than telling at all. Members will feel and often say, 'There's no way I can explain it to you.'" #10)

- **Members Experience "Peak Experiences"** ("Members will report 'peak experiences' in connection with their participation in the HPS. They will 'enthuse', 'bubble', communicate 'joy' and 'exultation.'" #12)

- **Performance Breakthroughs Occur in Unplanned Ways** ("Performance breakthroughs occur in unplanned ways. Hypothesis 12 will be especially obvious on these occasions. Members will account for the event in relatively non–operational idioms, such as 'we finally got it all together.'" #13)

- **External Controls Are Seen As Irrelevant—Never Look at the Clock** ("External controls on the activity of the HPS are seen by members as at best irrelevant and at worst as positive impediments to performance. Circumvention of the rules tends to be overt and non-apologetic." #17. Also #20: "Members seek relief from the pressures of participation in the HPS according to criteria which are internal to the system—its current phase of operations and the needs and expectations of other members. External schedules for relief and breaks are usually regarded by members as inappropriate.")

- **The System Is Always "ON"—Even If You Can't See It** ("The system does not have a clear OFF/ON character. Members may regard it as ON when it seems OFF to observers, and OFF when it seems ON. The system's movement from one state to the other is often difficult to detect from the outside." #19)

- **Neighboring Organizations Are Not Necessarily Pleased with HPS's Output.** ("The social value of the output of an HPS is problematic. Entities in the HPS's environment will not auto-matically be 'pleased' with its output." # 24)

- **Members May Be Perceived as Thrill Seekers, Weirdos, or Mystics** ("To the extent that members find participation in the HPS thrilling, they may become 'thrill seekers.' Activity in the HPS may provide a wide variety of sensual, affective, and cogni-tive experiences which, over time, members may become 'moti-vated' to attain and re-experience. For the most part, this kind of motivation may be relatively incomprehensible to observers. They may come to regard members so motivated as 'weirdoes' or 'mystics'. Negative judgments about members' maturity and even morality may be made by untrained observers." #34)

- **HPS's Groove** ("HPS's exhibit a rhythm of operation which is both subjectively felt by members and objectively evident to observers. An argot will exist for describing this rhythm, for example, 'tempo' (chess); 'footing' (yacht racing); 'wailing' (improvisational jazz); also 'getting it on' and 'grooving'—and note that 'grooving' has been extended in its application to many other activities; 'taking it to . . . (the opposing team)'; 'traction' (term coined by W. Baldamus to account for the tendency of an assembly line job to pull the worker along); 'hitting one's stride'; 'having a hot hand' (basketball); 'getting the boat set up' (crew); and 'mounting a charge' (golf). The general phenomenon that these terms refer to is that the same or improved effects are produced with substantially less effort than before the particular rhythm was achieved." #39)

In reviewing Vaill's Behavioral Characteristics of HPS's, it quickly becomes apparent that the organizations described are anything but "standard issue." Consider, for example, the characteristic, *Members May Be Perceived As Thrill Seekers, Weirdos, or Mystics*. And the other characteristics are scarcely better. The fact that members *Do Not Follow the Rule Book* is sufficient to drive any well-trained manager to distraction.

To the extent that Vaill's Characteristics accurately reflect the general behaviors and conditions of High Performing Systems—doing what they do with Excellence, it is perhaps not surprising that the search for excellence has often come up empty-handed.

And when it comes to our efforts to foster the development of such systems, our success just might have all of the popularity of a skunk at a garden party. It could turn out that although excellence and High Performance are valued in the abstract, the behavior of those who actually achieve these laudable states is socially unacceptable. Despite the odds, there can be little question that the search for both continues with intensity.

Chapter II

High Performance Systems Defined

Peter Vaill declined to define a High Performing System, which appears reasonable since we always seem to know one when we meet. It simply does better than the competition, and usually a lot better. Despite Vaill's hesitance I feel compelled to make some effort at definition, which may be yet another example of fools rushing in where angels fear to tread. However, I am not insensitive to the risks involved, and therefore have chosen to back into the task by starting with a definition that I know does not work.

High Performance Defined as the Absence of Its Opposites

It is tempting to define an HPS in terms of the absence of the apparent opposites, such things as chaos, confusion, and conflict. If only we could rid our systems of this trio then perhaps order, clear thinking, and peace would reign. Under these circumstances, high performance would appear to be inevitable, or at least clearly within our grasp.

There is some problem with this approach, however, in that all three of these (chaos, confusion, and conflict) seem to be essential to living, and therefore their elimination would do substantial damage to life, to say nothing of high performing life. For those of us who cherish a pacific lifestyle, such an assertion verges on the outrageous, but consider the following.

Chaos

The antidote for order, and most especially The Established Order—represents the dissolution of things as they were. It is always uncomfortable, not to say painful, but if we are ever going to experience novelty, space is required for the emergence of the new. Indeed scientists are now telling us that not only is chaos a part of life, a fact we know all too well, but that chaos is essential to life. Without chaos, there would be no life. Obviously this represents a distinct departure from that part of the conventional wisdom which perceives a meaningful life to be one of balance and equilibrium. However, as a biologist friend pointed out—when you reach equilibrium in biology, you are dead. The sad truth of the matter is that there is precisely one instant in our entire existence when we achieve equilibrium, and that is in the moment of our dying. Until then we are in some state of dis-equilibrium, and that is life.

Confusion

Confusion is the intellectual equivalent of chaos, and like chaos, it has gifts to give, albeit painful ones. Confusion serves the useful function of muddling made up minds so that new ideas may break through. It is always disconcerting when it happens, but as long as we are confirmed in our settled opinions, the likelihood of seeing our world in new, different, and better ways will elude us. The onset of confusion is typically marked by the perception of anomaly. Things just aren't working the way they are supposed to, and we are confronted with a choice. Perhaps our vision is impaired?

Or perhaps the spectacles through which we have been viewing our life need to be replaced? It is all very confusing, but when, and if, the day arrives in which the perceived anomaly is no longer the exception, we will have reached the cutting edge of new knowledge. It may just be that confusion is the beginning of wisdom.

Conflict

Conflict is annoying at the least and lethal at the worst, but it does have its uses. In the world of ideas, conflict provides the necessary abrasive qualities to smooth rough ideas into real gems. And conflict can also consign bad ideas to the trash heap. For sure there is destruction, and in the case of dearly held ideas, no small amount of pain. But the net gain for us as individuals and organizations is unquestionably worth the pain—most especially if we are to achieve optimal levels of performance. The ideal of an organization free from conflict is, in my judgment, a dog that won't hunt. In fact, if you will show me an organization without conflict, I will show you a dead one.

I submit that an understanding of a high performing system as being one in which chaos, confusion, and conflict have somehow been eliminated is a vain hope and a hollow shell, devoid of the very elements that make life and high performance possible. That the presence of the 3 C's is painful and destructive cannot be denied. However, the act of destruction is essential to their function, and the associated pain is an unfortunate consequence. All of which brings us to a fourth element which is typically understood as being antithetical to performance at all levels, and certainly High Performance. That fourth element is Ending, and perhaps even Death.

Ending and Death

The simple truth of the matter is that as chaos, confusion, and conflict do their work, things come and go, they end. We could say they die. For fairly obvious reasons, we as human beings are not particularly happy with this arrangement. However, as things stand it is a fact—for every beginning there is an end. For every life there is a death.

Beyond the fact that no matter our feelings and hopes, Death and Ending hold an inescapable place in our world. It is also true that both make a positive contribution in our journey toward High Performance. And to the extent that we deny them their rightful place we inhibit our capacity to perform at high levels. Although this may appear massively counterintuitive, think about it for a moment. When we hang on tenaciously to the way things are, we preclude the possibility of serious improvement. Current thoughts, current practices, current modes of life may be familiar and dear, but their continued embrace bars the way to future evolution.

Toward an Understanding of High Performance

Chaos, confusion, conflict, in addition the ending and death cannot be seen as the enemies of high performance, for each contributes in substantive, albeit painful, ways to the elevation of the human enterprise. The fact that we might wish it differently does not change the reality that the 3 C's and the Terminal Two come with the territory. Whatever understanding or definition of High Performance we may devise must not only include, but also transcend this troublesome quintet.

A Definition of High Performance

So how should we understand High Performance and define a High Performing System? I offer the following: *High Performance is the productive interplay of diverse, complex forces, including chaos, confusion, and conflict, and characterized by wholeness, health, and harmony.* It is *harmonious,* including all elements of harmony both consonance and dissonance, in that multiple forces work together to create a unitary flow. It is *whole* in the sense that there is a clear focus, direction, and purpose. It is *healthy* in that the toxins of its process (metabolic by-products in organisms) are eliminated effectively and without prejudice to itself or environment. High Performance can never be sustained at the cost of a fouled nest. A *High Performing System* is one that does all of the above with excellence, over time, and certainly better than comparable organizations.

Unpacking all of this will take some time, or more exactly the balance of this book. In the interim, and on the off chance that the relatively dry, academic definition may lack something when it comes to punch, permit me to offer an image. It is The River, the whole river in all of its seasons and places. And not just any river, but a mighty river coursing from its genesis to the sea, untrammeled by arbitrary barriers and boundaries, otherwise known as dams and levees.

Human beings seem to prefer domesticated rivers, but such rivers can never do their full work—and genuine high performance is not one of their characteristics. In addition to the placid interludes there are treacherous currents, wild rapids, occasional falls, and massive floods. There are warm days and cold days—days on which the humidity is so thick it must be cut with a knife, and other days when the chill winds of an arctic winter turn the massive flow into a solid state. The whole river, over its entire length, and through all of its days—doing its work reshaping and fertilizing the earth. That is my picture of High Performance.

Some 2600 years ago, the Chinese general, Sun Tsu, seems to have had a similar understanding. Writing in *The Art of War*, he said, "Thus the army does not maintain any constant strategic configuration of power, water has no constant shape. One who is able to change and transform in accord with the enemy and wrest victory is termed spiritual."[5] Of course the general is writing about armies and war, which may make some uncomfortable, but he clearly understood the power of flow. In short, this is not exactly a new idea.

Between Peter Vaill's Behavioral Characteristics, Sun Tzu's flowing water, and my attempts at definition, perhaps we now know what we're looking for. But the question remains—how do we get there from here?

---

5 Sun Tsu, *The Art of War* (Running Press, p. 61).

Chapter III

Getting from Here to There

Ff Excellence and High Performance are the objectives we seek, how do we get there from here? The short answer could be: Define the problem and fix it.

This simple approach has much to commend it. If nothing else it seems like the logical thing to do, and from this logical basis a rational approach to the achievement of High Performance surely emerges. So for example, if a business is suffering from diminished sales one would begin with a consideration of the relevant factors such as the general state of the market, the position of competitors, and eventually focusing on the sales mechanisms in the business itself. Should it turn out that the market is strong and that competing products have no special advantage, the problem is clearly internal. As pleasant and dedicated as our sales manager may appear, and even though the sales force is ever so energetic—a fix is required.

The fix could start with a simple upgrading of sales training, but if that does not bear immediate and positive results, the scalpel of change must cut deeper. Perhaps our friendly sales manager has passed her prime? And all those eager, energetic members of the sales force, could it be that they are mere sycophants playing out an old script, written in another age? If so the fix is clear: radical surgery and organ replacement.

On a clear and otherwise unremarkable day the organizational fabric is torn—and a profusion of pink slips decorate the landscape. The old order is ushered to the door, and a new sales department arises from the ashes. High hopes and expectations accompany the new sales people as they are welcomed—but the results were not quite as anticipated. It turns out that the old sales manager was effectively the corporate Soul, the repository of the history and traditions. She was also the person that newcomers turned to in times of need and confusion. Not that she possessed the latest in technical wizardry, but she had a warm heart. Now that was all gone. However, sales improved and the organization did better (for the moment), but felt a lot worse.

Of course this is just a story, and a made up one at that. But it is a story that has been told many times with variations. The problem was found and the fix initiated. And in terms of the identified problem, it was undeniable—the fix worked for a time. However, there were unintended consequences. We might also note in passing the leadership style usually associated with this approach to high performance: clear, decisive, command, and control. And in case of need, "Off with their heads." A caricature for sure, but a character who appears in many management sagas: The Leader.

Unintended Consequences

Mother Nature has taught us some painful lessons through unintended consequences. Consider the matter of floods. Everybody knows that floods are destructive of performance at all levels. Clearly this represents a major problem, and fortunately the fix is obvious. Simply build dams and levees to control the floods. End of problem.

Well, it is the end of problem until that wonderful day when Mother Nature and Old Man River conspire to teach us a lesson. On such a day the rains fall and the river rises, we might even say rages—rages against the artificial barriers and constraints placed in its way. It turns out that floodplains have a purpose. In the ordinary course of events, that lovely flat land adjacent to the river sits high and dry, but when the rains come, as they will, that broad expanse of unencumbered real estate provides a safety valve for the torrent of waters. The added water spreads out gently (relatively speaking), minimizing destructive currents, except in the river gorge itself. And when the rains cease, as they always have, the flood waters percolate slowly through the land, leaving a gift of fresh soil and new seeds of all sorts. The land is renewed, and the flowers and grasses bloom. And so it has been as long as rivers have run—until we saw a problem and applied a fix!

To be fair, our fix seems to keep our feet dry under some circumstances—but definitely not all circumstances! And when those circumstances become extreme we no longer have a flood spreading out, renewing a floodplain, we have a disaster with a name we all remember, like Katrina or Johnstown. The fix becomes the problem, and worse yet, it generates a whole host of new problems. It is all about unintended consequences.

The ancient and honorable problem/solution approach to the troubling aspects of life can be effective, and the leaders who implement it appear equally effective—in the short term. However, its effectiveness is strictly limited to those situations where the variables are few, known, and controllable. Difficulty arises when the approach is generalized to all of life, or where life is downsized (at least in our thinking) to that which is observable and under our control. Which adds up to pretty much the same thing. It is fashionable these days to seek more sophisticated approaches, a positive step I am sure. But I think it worthwhile noting just how often the old synaptic response kicks in: Define the Problem and Fix it. And almost inevitably the synaptic response lands us in the tangled woods of unintended consequences. We might avoid some of the pain were we to pause for the thought that the superficial simplicity could well hide a monster of complexity.

The Closed System Hoax

The simple problem/solution paradigm had its origin, I believe, in a day dominated by what I might call, the Closed System Hoax, yet another example of a good idea put to a bad use. The notion of a Closed System developed in the world of science as men and women of great integrity sought to tease out the "important" from the "variable," all in the pursuit of fundamental knowledge. Thus in a scientific experiment, it is most important to know that the observed results (whatever they might be) were the product of the forces under study, and not some itinerant variable. To raise the odds of success, great effort is devoted to "closing the system" thereby guarding against such vagrant variables. If one is studying an atomic reaction, walls of lead and concrete are constructed to shield the field of study. But even with the best of intention and effort, it is always recognized that the system is never fully closed. One simply hoped that the disturbance wrought by uncontrolled variables lay beneath the level of significance—and if that weren't the case—add more lead and concrete. But in any event, the system is never really closed. And in fact the idea of a "closed system" is purely a scientific conceit, useful in certain experimental circum-stances, but never to be confused with reality.

Somewhere along the line, as the field of Management made an attempt to assume the mantle of Science, and thereby become Management Science, the notion of a Closed System came along with the baggage. And that baggage was welcomed with enthusiasm. It appeared to those who managed the corporate enterprise that, if they were able to effectively close the system, they could rid them-selves of the gremlins of chance and uncertainty, thereby enabling extraordinary levels of efficiency, effectiveness, profitability—to say nothing of High Performance.

It must be acknowledged that the ideal (idol?) of Organization as a Closed System served us well, and the industrial power and accomplishments of the West are the apparent proof of the pud-ding. If nothing else, it seemed to work. And in areas of our world where turbulence and change are somehow constrained to minimal levels, it continues to work. However, those tranquil patches have dwindled to a precious few, typically found at the very margins of life. And even in those remaining areas of tranquility it is fair to ask whether the sense of protected security is a matter of percep-tion or the condition of reality.

If we are to believe the growing conclusions of those scientists who make chaos and complexity their field of study, the world we live in is definitely a restless place with massive interconnections and constant turbulence. Such a world would never permit a closed space where total control of errant variables is a possibility. And those who presume such a possibility are suffering from some degree of delusion. There are few, if any certainties in our lives, but one would seem to come pretty close: *There is no such thing as a closed system*, and no matter how hard we try, there never will be. From the beginning, the notion of a Closed System was a scientific conceit, useful in certain experimental circumstances, but never to be confused with reality. And if that confusion occurs you end up with bad science. And should that confusion spread to life in general, or organizations in particular, we find ourselves treading on very shaky ground. Although it is definitely nice to feel that we are in charge, we are in fact victims of the Hoax of Closed Systems.

The Whole Systems Approach

As the limitations of the "Define the Problem and Fix it" approach became clearer, wise heads determined that the key difficulty lay in the narrowness of our view. By restricting our attention to a single problem, and a single solution, we overlooked the fact that our organizations were a mass of interconnected elements. And further, that to change any one element implicitly changed them all. It was therefore essential to expand our horizons to include the whole system. Ably led by Peter Senge[6] and a host of others, we did our best to adopt what has become known as Systemic Thinking.

The thought is glorious, albeit overwhelming. As we approach the task of optimizing our systems (organizations) in pursuit of true High Performance, we must consider all the pieces, in addition to identifying and understanding the complex interrelationships between any and all. It turns out that the components of our organizations (sales, marketing, finance, etc.—and all their subsets)

---

6 Peter Senge, *The Fifth Discipline* (Doubleday Currency, 1990).

are not good or bad, effective or ineffective in some abstract sense—but always in a context, a context determined by all the other related elements. So, for example, an outstanding Sales Department in one business cannot simply be bolted on to another business with any particular expectation that it will continue to be outstanding. It all depends. . .

In a way, The Whole Systems Approach is merely the old problem/solution approach writ large. We now have a humongous problem (the whole system), and any solution will undoubtedly be very detailed and complex. But the way forward seems clear enough. We must now describe and understand the system in its entirety (elements and relationships) before any attempt at a "fix." And the "fix" must be a paragon of elegance, taking into account an infinity of elements and connections. First step: Map the System.

Efforts at mapping the system(s) have been prodigious, producing dense diagrams of elements and connections all decorated with wondrous feedback and feedforward loops. As an academic exercise the enterprise has been more than worthwhile, for we have learned an enormous amount concerning the nature and complexity of our organizations and the operative dynamics. However, when it comes to the second step—the move from diagnosis to treatment, the results to date have been less than outstanding.

Process Re-Engineering

One of the major applications of Systems Thinking to the practical issue of fostering the development of high performance is Business Process Re-Engineering (BPR)[7]. Created by Michael

---

7 Michael Hammer and James Champy, *Re-Engineering the Corporation* (Harper Business, 2003).

Hammer and James Champy in the 90s, Process Re-Engineering proposed to map the total process of an organization and then carefully re-design it to create optimum efficiency.

There is no question that such a microscopic examination of current business practices was a valuable undertaking, but when it came to execution, the results very often did not seem to justify the effort expended. The fly in the ointment is our old friend, The Closed System Hoax. A tacit assumption of those involved seems to have been that while the lengthy, detailed analysis and design work was undertaken, the system under consideration could some-how be isolated from the larger world so that analysis performed at a given point in time would remain valid over time.

For example, in the 90s I had occasion to work with the American telephone company then known as USWEST. For several years they had been engaged in a massive BSR effort, and by the time I made their acquaintance, they were at that magical point of "throwing the switch"—turning on the new creation. However things were not going as predicted. Actually, it looked like immi-nent disaster, a fact made clear by a visit to their central control room in Denver, Colorado.

The function of that control room was to monitor and manage the whole system. And like many other such control rooms, system status was indicated by a series of color codes: Green–OK, Yellow–Caution, Red–Danger. On my visit the ambient lighting was mas-sively Red! The danger of the situation was reflected in some painful facts: at that point it was taking 6–9 months for the installation of a single telephone line. Even so–called Emergency Lines were taking a month or more. One engineer told me that if one more phone were plugged in, the whole system could crash. Somehow or another the re-engineered business was not doing too well.

The explanation that I was given for the critical situation had to do with earthquakes in California. In the mid 90s the San Andreas Fault slipped massively, producing catastrophic results from San Francisco to Los Angeles. Probably most Californians took the chaos in their stride or did not have any options, but a significant number found the shaking of their real estate not to their liking and decided to move. Those who took that decision were not without financial resources, and their destinations were anywhere but California, just not too far away. And so the contiguous states of Arizona, New Mexico, Nevada, Oregon, and Washington became the objectives of their flight. And these states just happened to be the service area of USWEST.

Upon arrival the Californians settled in accommodations matching their lifestyles and they wanted phones—lots of phones. A main line, a children's line, a computer line, a fax line, and spare lines as well—and they had the financial resources to pay for their desires. Unfortunately USWEST did not have the added capacity to meet those desires. That was not part of the plan, and hence the imminent disaster. It became apparent that the world had changed once again, and the system was anything but closed.

The example of USWEST may be an extreme one, and for sure a "whole system's approach" has much to commend it, but it is an open question as to whether we actually have the capacity to map the system in sufficient detail to picture the finer components and their inner working. Should we seek to better the odds of our success by cutting the system down to a size, we might reasonably handle by tacitly assuming a closed system, we leave ourselves vulnerable to a changing world which has the nasty habit of voiding our best laid plans. Lastly, if the chaos/complexity researchers are correct, that very minimal changes within, or adjacent to, the system can have massive impact (a butterfly changing the weather patterns in California with a wing flap, for example), the odds for a successful outcome in our enterprise grow exceedingly long. The concept, however, is marvelous even though its execution may be flawed. And of course, there is a nagging question—Have we really thought of the WHOLE system?

Have We Really Thought About the WHOLE System?

Ken Wilber, American psychologist, philosopher, and some would say mystic, would say no. Wilber is prone to making disarmingly simple and alarmingly profound observations. One of his best is, *Every inside has an outside and vice versa.* The point may be obvious, but we forget it to our detriment. In reference to human beings as individuals and as systems, Wilber reminds us that in addition to the exterior attributes, that which we can see touch, taste, or smell—there is a lot going on inside. An individual may be 5'2", eyes of blue, and skin of whatever shade. That information, however, tells us nothing about how they are feeling, how they see the world, how they see themselves, or what their hopes or aspirations might be. The situation is similar with an organization. We may see the plant and facilities, count the products produced, and employees on the payroll, but we remain in the dark when it comes to the organization's mythology, ritual, culture, shared but secret values, or the spirit of the place, be that soaring or sour.

Based upon his sim-
ple observation, Wilber
proposes that when
thinking about a system
and its constituent indi-
viduals, we should use
what he calls the Four
Quadrants[8] (see figure) as
a template to direct our
attention to all that lies

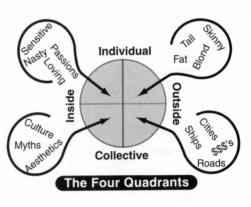

beneath the surface. Admittedly, following the Four Quadrants significantly increases the difficulty of thinking systemically if only
because the nature and scope of the system have been radically
expanded. But it strikes me that Wilber's logic is impeccable. For
example, if we see 100 individuals hard at work in a munitions fac-
tory, we can certainly measure the square footage of the shop floor,
identify the available machinery, count the bullets as they come off
the assembly line, calculate the potential profit, and thereby make
some judgment about the nature and effectiveness of the system.
However, until we have some reasonable understanding of what is
going on inside—how they feel about their work, what is their ideology, culture, special stories, or myths—we are largely in the dark
about the true nature of this "system." The fact that feelings, culture,
myth, and ideology are not easily quantifiable constitutes a genuine problem for our systems analysis, but detracts not a whit from
their importance to systems function.

---

8 Ken Wilber, *A Theory of Everything* (Shambala Publications, 2000).

Apparently we do very well with the hard, countable facts, however, our level of performance leaves something to be desired when it comes to what might be called the "warm fuzzies." And if we are serious about thinking and working systemically we must take the *whole* system into consideration. And it gets worse.

The "Worse"—Every System Has a Context

Unless we are to remain hostage to what I have called The Closed System Hoax we will have to confront the fact that no system, no matter what we do, is hermetically sealed. Every system, regardless of size, design, or purpose has a context, which is quite simply the planet on which we all live—all 6.5 billion of us. It is nice, perhaps comforting, to think that there are boundaries and barriers, but in truth they are largely arbitrary and always permeable. The fact that much of the interchange between the system and its context/surroundings occurs beneath our capacity to notice changes nothing in terms of impact.

None of this is exactly news. Our morning newspapers teach us these lessons on a daily basis at the breakfast table, and all but the most myopic must understand the incredible permeability of our world and its people. Every element relates to all other elements, if not immediately, then soon. But what is common knowledge at the breakfast table is seemingly laid to one side when it comes to the truly important business of understanding our systems and enhancing their effectiveness in pursuit of High Performance.

The Final Straw—Everything Is Moving!

The complex interrelationships that exist between any of our Human Systems and the world surrounding them are mind-boggling in their detail, however, it is at least conceivable that given sufficient time we might track them down. And if we could, the possibility exists that we could create an adequate map of the territory, sufficient to initiate the design or redesign process. We would at least know where we are starting. But there is an additional fly in the ointment. Not only is everything radically connected, but it is all moving, and with every move the nature and impact of the interrelationships can change. Worse yet, the rate of movement is random and differential. The final picture looks like something straight out of Alice in Wonderland, viewed in a carnival mirror. In recent time, the speed of movement is increasing at quantum rates. What once appeared as a rock of stability is now seen to be a firestorm of largely unpredictable activity. Whatever the cause, we are experiencing what I call "raplexity"—a neologism created from the words "rapid" and "complexity." We might deal with one or the other, but both together are productive of a headache of infinite proportions. Alvin Toffler, who gave us *Future Shock*[9], would be proud.

We Need Some Help

It might be assumed that I am dismissive of the systems approach in general, and Systems Thinking in particular. Nothing could be

9 Alvin Toffler, *Future Shock* (Random House, 1970).

further from the truth. Our new awareness of systems, their complexity, and modes of operations is a major advance. Those who
have pursued this particular adventure should be praised for their
skill, fortitude, and persistence. However, to the extent that this
massive effort was undertaken with the expectation that we might
design, and sustain, effective High Performing Systems, I think the
results to date are not encouraging. If anything our search for solutions of the sort anticipated has demonstrated the futility of search
itself. In short, we can't quite get there from here, at least going the
way we are going. We are, however, gaining a much clearer understanding of the sorts of attitudes and skills that are necessary if we
are going to perform the task we have undertaken. With some
degree of tongue in cheek, I offer the following job description of
that person who would create, on a sustained and sustainable
basis, true High Performing Systems, usually called The Leader.

Job Description: The Leader

Deals easily with massive diversity

Comprehends mind-bending complexity

Works simultaneously on multiple levels

Rises above chaos, confusion, and conflict

Tolerates tidal waves of change

Never loses their cool

Always in control

Mixes all of the above to produce wholeness,

health, and harmony

To the extent that this job description accurately reflects the
task at hand it is the job description from Hell. Given our current

abilities and the resources at hand, adequate performance is an exercise in futility. Great idea, but simply off the charts! Of course we might gain some traction were it possible to cut the task down to our size, which is what the Closed System Hoax purports to do. However, if we look honestly at the scope and complexity of the systems of our world, even very small ones, the proposed task makes putting Humpty Dumpty together again seem like a piece of cake. And for those of you who may not remember the children's ode to the fractured egg, it goes like this:

> Humpty Dumpty sat on a wall.
> Humpty Dumpty had a great fall.
> And all the King's horses
> And all the King's men
> Couldn't put Humpty together again.

What all the King's horses and all the King's men failed to accomplish is viewed by some of us as the central task of leadership, and most particularly The Great Man as leader. And the job description from Hell becomes effectively the short list of qualifications sought in our leaders. Is it any wonder that those who claim to possess such qualification, and even worse, seek to demonstrate them, burn out very quickly? Executive exhaustion, measured by exceedingly short half lives is not surprising. What is surprising is that any sane individual would make the attempt. If we are currently experiencing a shortage of leadership in the mold of The Great Man, it could be that a breath of sanity has crossed our organizations. Fewer people are rushing to accept the mission—which is clearly a Mission Impossible.

We are dealing with something of such magnitude, complexity, and changeability that even thinking about it creates massive overload. And of course, what you can't even think about renders the task of doing something useful all but impossible, and tight control is out of the question. Obviously many people have tried, and in fact the fruits of their labors, in terms of a deeper understanding of the mechanisms and magnitude of our systems, have been substantial. But when it comes to the task of putting all the pieces together to design, create, and sustain truly High Performing Systems, I believe it safe to say that we could use some serious help.

Chapter IV

The Anomalies

For all of our searching for High Performing Systems, it turns out that they are very much present, hiding in plain sight. It is just that they are rarely where we might expect them, certainly do not appear when we want them—and even less when we planned on their arrival. Most usually, the High Performing Systems in our midst pop up as curious anomalies in the larger fabric of our enterprise.

The actual stories are legion. My personal favorite is the tale of *Post-its*—the omnipresent product of the 3M corporation. To hear the current corporate version of the story, one could draw the conclusion that the little yellow (now multi-colored) "stickies" came to market by way of a concerted corporate effort made in an atmosphere of broad support for innovation. If you listen to the tale as told by those who were there at the creation, the situation was a little bit different.

The story begins, as I have heard it from several of the perpetrators, with a curious mistake. It seems that one of the 3M chemists, working in the area of adhesives, came up with a glue that was perpetually sticky—not exactly the sort of performance one might prefer. What happened next is a matter of some confusion in my mind, but either the chemist himself, or a friend, just happened to sing in a choir. In that choir it was common practice to page mark all the hymns to be sung during the service with little slips of paper. This was a workable solution until the slips of paper fell out of the books—which they always seemed to do at the most inopportune times. Needed: a practical way of holding the papers in place without permanent attachment. Solution: a perpetually sticky, but easily removable, glue.

And so it occurred that the chemist's little mistake had a potential use. And when that use was attempted the result was a total success. Not only did the errant papers not fall from the hymnals, but all members of the choir wanted their own pad of sticky markers. It would seem that a new product had been born. However, the trail from genesis to the general market was not a straight one.

The sticky markers attracted an odd group of adherents—a small random assemblage of 3M people who were united only by the fact that they cared about the stickies and their potential. Nobody "worked" for anybody else, and if there was a Development Plan, nobody ever saw it. But without a plan or formal structure, the product evolved and improved. New uses were imagined and the appearance and effectiveness were enhanced. What began as a hymnal page marker became the familiar sticky notepad appearing in a rainbow of colors and multiple sizes and shapes.

Perhaps most remarkable, none of this took place with the official imprimatur of 3M. In fact, just the opposite. The corporate powers did their best to first ignore, and then suppress the now popular Post-it, to the point that the dedicated band of developers had to work secretly, in off hours, using "borrowed" resources. And when it came to scaling up the effort, it is said that the original capital came from the piggy banks of those who cared. Eventually, of course, 3M had to face the obvious. They had a runaway best seller, but all of that was never a part of The Plan.

Whether or not the Post-it story clearly meets Peter Vaill's defining characteristics of a High Performing System could be a matter of debate, but there is little question that this dedicated crew had all the earmarks of what Tom Peters described as a skunkworks. Out of sight, out of mind, definitely not popular (with the powers that be), and frightfully productive—but never according to The Plan. And I would argue that the correlation with Peter Vaill's "intuitive leaps" is also very high. There is no question that the Rule Book was not followed, and equally no doubt that "Performance breakthroughs occurred in unplanned ways." And surely, the neighboring organization (3M) was not pleased with the HPS's output. Whether the members actually all experienced "peak experiences," I can't say for sure, but the individual who told me the tale, and was part of the original circle—described that time in his professional career as life changing and one of the best moments of his experience. One thing I am quite sure of, however, is that from the point of view of the corporate hierarchy, the members were definitely seen as "weirdos and mystics," even if those words were never actually used.

The tale of Post-its has now passed into corporate lore as a delightful example of those anomalous, serendipitous, breakthrough moments which spice up the otherwise drab and predictable life in a business organization. Definitely one of a kind, and rarely to be repeated—at least that is the story. But I am not so sure that story is correct. In fact, I strongly suspect that HPS breakthrough is, if not an everyday, then at least a common occurrence—which is usually not noticed, or if noticed then marginalized, because it does not fit the template of our expectations. It is very hard to see something that you are not expecting, and even harder when you "know" that it could not, or should not, take place. The relative prevalence, and our difficulty in perceiving HPS's when they do appear, is highlighted in this curious tale from the Dupont Corporation.

Breaking Through at Dupont

The Dupont Corporation is one of the United States' oldest and largest. It is known for many familiar products, but perhaps more than the products produced, Dupont is known for its emphasis on research, and more particularly, for its own "brand" of research— which it called, Programed Research. One might view Programed Research as an early version of what is now known as Knowledge Management, for the people at Dupont felt that it was both possible and desirable to treat research and the knowledge generated in much the same way they would treat any other asset. And so they created Research Portfolios containing good ideas worthy of development—along with a procedure (Programed Research) for getting all that done.

Some years ago, I was retained to assist one of the Dupont units (the people who made Dacron) to achieve what they had called "Breakthrough Research." As we started on this adventure, I thought it well to attempt some sort of benchmarking. Thus in a meeting with all the research directors associated with Dacron, I asked what I considered to be a very basic question, "Had they ever had a breakthrough?" After some thought they said there had been six. I did not press for the details if only because I knew that the mysteries of polymer chemistry were well beyond my capacity for understanding. However, I did ask another question, which for me went to the heart of the matter. "How many of these break-throughs occurred in accordance with The Plan, otherwise known as Programed Research?" Their answer was very slow in coming, I suspect, because none of them really wanted to admit that the central pillars of their research effort had occurred in ways quite unrelated to what was supposed to be the official path to knowl-edge. The answer was "zero."

It is fair to ask whether these six breakthroughs were all the products of High Performing Systems, and the truthful answer is that I really don't know—but it seemed to me that a number of the significant characteristics were present, not the least of which was that all had occurred in unplanned ways. In several instances where I was able to gather some of the details of genesis, other characteristics showed up. The groups involved with the discovery were typically not formal work groups, and they clearly had a light regard for the official corporate rules of research. They apparently worked at odd hours (didn't check the clock), and with great enthusiasm. None of the members were described as "mystics or weirdos," but such words would not come naturally to the rather reserved polymer chemists of Dupont. However, there was no question that the members were seen to have wandered quite off the beaten path.

What I found particularly interesting was the amount of time it took before this group of laboratory directors actually recognized the breakthroughs they had achieved. I take this as an example of the power of the templates of our minds which tell us how things ought to be. And when reality fails to fit the template, it is often passed by unnoticed. The point is a simple one: The prevalence of true High Performing Systems is probably much higher than we might expect. This, however, does not obviate a very substantial issue. The High Performing Systems that we encounter typically appear in unexpected times and places, and rarely according to The Plan. Could we change this? Is it possible to achieve High Performance on demand?

A Hopeful Tale

In 1995, AT&T, along with other large corporations, was preparing plans for their pavilion in the Global Village of the 1996 Olympics to be held in Atlanta. An outstanding team of 23 architects, exhibit designers, public relations folks, and security experts had been assembled for the task, and they had been hard at work over a 10-month period. By the early fall, the plans were essentially complete and construction was soon to begin on the $200 million structure.

At that point a wonderful opportunity with disastrous implications emerged. The Olympic Committee was so impressed with the AT&T design that they invited the corporation to consider moving its pavilion from its currently assigned location at the edge of the Global Village to the very center. Since AT&T was contemplating the expenditure of $200 million with but a single purpose in mind, exposure—accepting the committee's invitation was irresistible. But there was a difficulty. At the edge of the Global Village, one might anticipate 5000 visitors a day. At the very center, the expected number of visitors exploded to 75,000. Obviously a structure designed for 5000 would be grossly inadequate for 75,000, and even worse, time was running out. The decision to move was made in November and the Olympics effectively start in June, at least you have to have your buildings in place. It had previously taken 10 months to do the old design and scarcely 7 months remained in which to do both the design and construction. In addition, Christmas and New Years were about to put in an appearance, taking further time off the clock.

The design team was invited to a two day meeting outside of New York City. As they entered the conference room, they found a circle of empty chairs waiting for them. On a blank wall behind the chairs were posted several hand lettered signs bearing the titles, "The Four Principles" and "The Law of Two Feet." The Four Principles, expressed in terse, colloquial terms, read as follows: Whoever comes are the right people. Whatever happens is the only thing that could have. Whenever it starts is the right time. When it is over it is over. The Law of Two Feet was not even outlined. Even worse there was not a shred of agenda, and zero indication of what might happen next.

To say that this design team was in some condition of agitation would be an understatement. They knew they possessed the competence to do the job, if only because they had done it before. They also knew that the time available rendered the completion of the task virtually impossible. Then to be thrown into this totally weird situation of sitting in a circle gazing at their peers and colleagues across an empty space—and anxiety quickly became pure outrage. This outrage was hardly mollified when a gentleman none had ever seen before walked to the edge of the circle and said, "Welcome to Open Space."

What happened next, and over the following two days, was vastly different from what might have been predicted. Within an hour of start, the group had identified all of the issues and opportunities they perceived as having an impact on the performance of their task. And half an hour later ($1\frac{1}{2}$ hours from start) they were deeply engaged in multiple subgroups working the identified issues, pausing only for a cup of coffee, a quick meal, or to write up their conclusions on nearby computers. Whatever questions there may have been at the beginning were quickly overwhelmed in a firestorm of productive activity.

As the second day commenced the activity continued, but with a difference. The defined groups dissolved into each other as participants moved with seeming randomness from one area of discussion to another, or stopped along the way for new conversations that somehow had not made it into the original agenda. The atmosphere itself was radically altered, as laughter broke out in the midst of arduous work, and random conversations yielded unpredictable results. For example, one of the participants who had been responsible for lighting in the Grateful Dead concerts was overheard in serious conversation with the security consultant on the possibility of using lasers to somehow combat potential terrorists.

To an outside observer, the scene was one of total chaos and confusion. The ambient energy was virtually overwhelming, and the logic of its passage far from clear. It would hardly be an overstatement to say that the design process had gone into flow state in which the borders of the work groups merged seamlessly. Whatever schedule had existed simply disappeared, time and clocks were irrelevant. If anybody was in charge, that person was totally invisible.

At 5:00 pm on the final day, or thereabouts, all visible activity ceased, and for a moment, there was silence. It was not the silence of exhaustion, but satisfaction. The group had done it! A new design had been created, not just as a vague concept, but in sub-stantive form all laid out in working architectural drawings. These drawings were not pretty, and work remained in terms of filling out the details, but the plan existed, and the way forward was clear. And there was more. The group agreed that not only was the design functional (able to handle the expected 75,000 visitors), but that aesthetically it represented a vast improvement over its prede-cessor. In addition, they were actually further ahead with imple-mentation of the new design than they had been with the old one. As they were working in New York, they were glued to their cell phones, ordering up supplies and materials for the job. And last, but by no means least, all 23 participants were still talking to each other. This may seem a small point, but such intense effort is often productive of frayed tempers. To be sure there had been no lack of spirited engagement and at moments, hot conflict, but somehow that had all resolved and resulted in an improved product.

I think it fair to say that the activities and experience of those 23 individuals constituted a High Performing System in action. At a substantive level, the output exceeded all expectations, and certain-ly the expectations of the group. They had done in two days what, on the basis of prior experience, everybody knew was going to take 10 months. Measured as an increase in productivity, that rep-resents something like a 15,000% addition. And seen from the point of view of Peter Vaill's Behavioral Characteristics, it would appear that they were all present and accounted for. Clearly everybody forgot the Rule Book, if it ever existed. And in fact it did exist, for within broad limits there is an accepted practice as to how one goes about designing large buildings. When it comes to external prompts, such things as clocks and managerial direction, neither were in evidence, and if they were, nobody paid any attention. And of course, the almost incandescent flow state which the group achieved was pure "grooving," by whatever name. Since this was an individual, one time meeting, with no particular and long lasting relationship to surrounding systems, it is unclear what such systems might have thought about their output. Although in this regard, it is interesting that following the meeting I was told that some complaints (maybe better, "grumbles") arose from other parts of the AT&T system which suddenly found the whole timetable speeded up. What they had thought might be a requirement in March or April suddenly hit the front burner in January or February. As for "members enthusing" that was clearly the case. Russ Natoce, AT&T executive who bore responsibility for the Pavilion, was overheard mumbling, "It's magic, It's magic."

High Performing Systems in Our Midst

My three stories prove nothing, but proof was never the intention. In describing a few of the multiple "HPS appearances" in my own experience, it is my hope that you the reader might be drawn to consider your own experience. If as I suspect, you also find High Performance (Systems) appearing with some regularity in odd times and places, my intention will have been fulfilled. We might then agree that HPS's show up more often than one might suppose, although their appearance is often veiled by the fact that they do not show up in the form and fashion we would expect. They arrive unplanned for, involve people we might never suspect, and carry out their business in a fashion that does not coincide with standard practice. In short they appear as anomalies, which are very easy to discount or totally overlook. However, when anomalous behavior shows up in regular and comparable patterns, there may well be more going on than meets the eye.

Two of the HPS examples (Dupont and 3M) were what might be called "natural occurrences." There was no intention to do anything out of the ordinary—it just seemed to happen. The third example is rather different. In that case, the people at AT&T needed a minor miracle, and proceeded to find it in a most curious fashion. A simple process enabled high performance at surprising levels, with concrete results well beyond the expectations of the participant group. As one of the members said, "It's magic."

What may have seemed magical in that moment was a very ordinary application of Open Space Technology. The conventional practice and theory of organization would find it difficult to understand how a group of talented professionals might move from a circle of outraged confusion to active and productive engagement, without benefit of an agenda, prior training, and intense facilitation. And yet, in less than an hour and a half the group was seriously at work, and 48 hours later, they had surpassed their expectations. Had this experience been a one time thing, we might reasonably suspect divine intervention, mass hallucination, or indeed magic. However, as of this writing, that experience has been repeated on multiple occasions. Not every instance produced such dramatic and clear-cut results, but the results have been comparable in all instances, provided that the initial conditions were appropriate, and the process followed. It would appear that the achievement of high performance on some regular, and even predictable basis, may be within our grasp.

Chapter V

The Open Space Experiment

O pen Space Technology was first developed and utilized in 1985. At the point of genesis there was no thought to run any sort of an experiment. In fact, the precipitating condition was a very practical need. Open Space Technology emerged as an intuitive response. It took five years before it became apparent that a grand natural experiment was in progress. But that is to get considerably ahead of the story.

The story begins on a warm afternoon in April 1985—the first real day of spring in Washington, DC. In celebration of the season, I went to my patio with my first "outdoors" martini in hand. As I savored the drink, a disturbing thought passed through my mind. I had agreed to convene a symposium set for early July, dealing with Organization Transformation, to which I had given little thought.

I had convened the first of such gatherings two years earlier, and by any reasonable standard it had been quite a success. The participants, however, let it be known that even though they had enjoyed the various speakers and panels, the most useful and productive parts of the entire event were the coffee breaks. I found myself in agreement.

For the participants the fond memories of the coffee breaks were perhaps an incidental thought. For me those memories constituted a painful awakening. As the convener of the symposium I had spent the better part of a year arranging for speakers and panels. To be faced with the fact that all my efforts had basically produced interruptions to the most productive and enjoyable aspect of the entire affair was, to say the least, disturbing.

Pouring a second martini, I found myself falling into a reverie. Images unasked wandered into my head. The first image came from a time I worked in West Africa. I noticed that when the people had a serious issue to resolve they invariably sat in a circle. I thought that might be a reasonable place to start with our symposium—sit in a circle. But passive presence in a circle does not a symposium make. What will we talk about? A second image came to the fore—a bulletin board. We could simply post our topics of interest on a bulletin board. And that would leave only the practicalities of time, place, and participants. Where and when would the interested parties meet? The final image provided an answer. It was of an indigenous marketplace where people gathered freely at little stalls to buy, sell, and exchange the news of the day.

And there it was: Sit in a circle, create a bulletin board, open a marketplace, and go to work. Four months later 85 brave souls gathered in Monterey, California, for the Third International Symposium on Organization Transformation. There was no agenda, no planning committee, and virtually nothing by way of overt leadership.

The initial running of Open Space Technology was hardly an earth shattering event. Over the next four years, the level of notice scarcely increased. The Annual International Symposium on Organization Transformation occurred with regularity, and always took place in Open Space. The number of participants increased and the time required from start to the opening of the first sessions decreased, but none of that seemed particularly noteworthy. There actually came a time when I found myself becoming bored with the whole business. After all, as the facilitator I did virtually nothing and it seemed that the less I did, the better things worked. Talk about working yourself out of a job!

My boredom ended abruptly in 1989 when a client, the Dacron Research team of the Dupont Corporation, found itself in the sticky situation I described above. Market forces and historical circumstances produced a set of conditions which required what my client described as "Breakthrough Research." And this was Breakthrough Research on a very short timetable. The applicable patents were about to expire, and other corporations had the capacity to manufacture Dacron faster and cheaper than its inventor, Dupont. The core question was—should they just leave the business? The answer seemed to be an inescapable, yes—unless ways could be found to produce the product that were better and different—all on a very short timetable.

When asked for my opinion, I found myself in something of a quandary. I thought I knew how to approach the issue over time, but not in the short time available. And the only thing that came to my mind was that funny approach we had been using for our symposia—Open Space Technology. I mentioned the possibility to my client with the caveat that although I thought it could work, I had never actually used it in what was obviously a real, critical, business situation. Discretion would dictate a fierce search for alternatives, with OST being a possible, but virtually untested option.

As things turned out, we ran out of alternatives, and on the appointed day 175 polymer chemists found themselves sitting in a circle, creating a bulletin board, opening a marketplace—and getting on with the business of re-inventing Dacron.

I can't honestly say that all technical problems were resolved in that OST, but I do know that there was an extraordinary level of interaction during the event, which matched in detail the behavioral characteristic enumerated by Peter Vaill, and that by the conclusion, the participants seemed well pleased with their accomplishments. The fact that Dacron continues in the Dupont product line suggests that what had been initiated on that day bore fruit.

The Cure for Boredom and the Beginning of the Grand Experiment

In the aftermath of my experience with Dupont I found myself in a very curious good news / bad news situation. The good news is pretty obvious—the long shot bet on OST had paid off. But the bad news, or at least the troubling news, was that I did not have a clue as to why it worked. Worse still, what we had done violated virtually every single principle and practice I considered to be self-evident and true when it came to the management of meetings and organizations. Everybody "knew," myself included, that dealing with an issue of such magnitude and complexity required careful agenda preparation, intense facilitation, and prior training for the participants. We had done none of that. It seemed that we had an anomaly within an anomaly—but it was far from boring.

Over time it occurred to me that we had the makings of a wonderful natural experiment. We had definable experimental conditions (see below), a prescribed procedure—and with time, we would surely come to some experimental results. But what was the

hypothesis? And perhaps even more curious—what was the underlying mechanism?

The advantage of a natural experiment is that explorations are
possible which might otherwise be prohibited because of cost,
feasability, or even ethics. However, since the experiment is "running" all by itself, we may take advantage of that fact to learn something. The disadvantage of a natural experiment is that, because it
was totally unplanned (at least as an experiment), all of the usual
safeguards and protocols are not in place. This deficiency creates
problems when it comes to confidence in the results. Open Space
Technology was just about as "unplanned" as you can get, and definitely never thought of as an experiment. However, when a natural
experiment reaches a certain size and duration, the simple force of
numbers may help to overcome questions of validity. In the case of
OST there is now a 22-year experience with something in excess of
100,000 applications in over 136 countries, facilitated by several
thousand different facilitators. With that level of experience it may
be confidently stated that something interesting is taking place.

The Experimental Conditions

In the early days of OST, as more and more people heard about it,
I was often asked what were the appropriate conditions for use.
Growing experience taught me that the following were essential:
(1) *A "real" business issue*—In other words it was important that the
initiating issue be something that people really care about. Just
going through the motions without that galvanizing issue pro-
duces little more than a yawn. (2) *Voluntary self-selection*—It is important that those who attend do so because they *cared* to come, and

not because they were ordered or commanded to do so. Voluntary self-selection in response to a genuine invitation (an invitation which can be refused) is critical. (3) *High levels of complexity*—The issue itself must be a complex one such that no single person, or even a group of people, could effectively untangle the details and work for a solution. (4) *High levels of diversity*—Diversity refers here to the participating group. If the participants are generally homogeneous OST will work, but not nearly as effectively as when there are vast differences within the group in whatever way "difference" may be measured, including ethnicity, gender, profession, life experience, economics, to name a few. Contrary to the conventional view that limiting diversity will increase the probability of a successful outcome—in OST the exact opposite is true. (5) *Presence of passion and conflict*—Actually passion and conflict are two sides of the same coin, for conflict occurs when two or more passions engage each other without sufficient space to maneuver. Obviously the conflict could be eliminated by removing the passions, but then the whole enterprise would be dead in the water. (6) *A decision time of yesterday*—There must be some real sense of urgency, and doing an OST around an issue that may come due in 20 years is bland to the point of dysfunction.

These conditions were developed as criteria for the use/nonuse of OST, but as my experience became much more one of participating in an ongoing natural experiment, they assumed the role of experimental conditions. The conditions are not absolute in the sense that they must be present at some predetermined level, but all are essential, and the higher the level of their presence the more productive the OST.

The Procedure

I have already outlined the fundamental elements of the procedure—sit in a circle, create a bulletin board, open a market-place, and go to work. And it really is just that simple, however a few additional details may round out the picture, although they do not change it in any substantial way.

While the participants are sitting in the circle, they are invited (not commanded) to identify any issue related to the business at hand, for which they have real passion and are willing to take per-sonal responsibility. Open Space is not brainstorming where people think of good ideas for somebody else to do. In Open Space the issues are those that people care about, to the point that they will take personal responsibility to get something useful accomplished. These issues become the agenda, and passion and responsibility provide the essential ingredients to ensure that the issues are care-fully addressed and (if possible) acted upon.

While the participants are considering possible issues, the facil-itator will describe four principles and one law. The Four Principles are as follows: (1) *Whoever comes is the right people.* This principle reminds participants that when they get into their discussion groups whoever chooses to join them will be precisely the right people for the discussion. What makes them the "right" people is simply that they care sufficiently about the issue at hand to come. *Caring* is the critical factor even though every participant may care in different ways. (2) *Whatever happens is the only thing that could have.* This principle focuses attention in the moment and reminds people that all the "might have beens, could have beens, or should have beens" have no practical impact in that moment. What *is*—is the only game in town in that moment. (3) *Whenever it starts is the right time.* A principle to drive conscientious managers crazy, but essential for all of that. The point is really about creativity and innovation which always happen when they are ready, and never a moment before—regardless of what the clock may say. (4) *When it is over it is over.* The final principle merely states the obvious, everything has an end, and when that end arrives, it is time to move on. Practically in an OST this means that when a discussion has covered the territory, even if it has not filled the time allotted, it is useful to do something else. In short, don't waste time.

The one law, which we have called the Law of Two Feet is very direct: *If you find yourself in any situation in which you are neither learning nor contributing, use your two feet and move to some better place.* Upon first hearing, many people find the law to be unsettling, even rude. After all, we have all been taught that it is impolite to leave just because you are bored. In a work situation it is presumed that if everybody just followed their feet, little if anything would get done. And yet in an OST environment it becomes very clear that the efficiency, effectiveness, and overall productivity of the gathering vary directly with the observance of the law. In a word, when feet are moving, positive things happen.

I mentioned above that while the recitation of the principles and the law constitute an element in the procedure of OST—and perhaps even a noteworthy element, they do not change the procedure in any substantial way. This is because both the principles and the law are fundamentally *descriptive* as opposed to prescriptive. They describe what will be the case in any event, even if unmentioned.

This is even true of the Law of Two Feet. It is a common experience, shared by all of us, that when we encounter situations where we are neither learning nor contributing, we leave—if not physically then mentally and emotionally. It might appear that sitting inertly in the corner would be the proper thing to do, but our continued (physical) presence is rarely if ever inert. We impact the conversation, and usually in a negative fashion. Our bored, frustrated demeanor spews negative energy over the entire affair. Much better that we actually allow our feet to follow our hearts and minds and just leave.

Experimental Results

The particular outcomes of the multiple OST events I have facilitated, or participated in, over the past 20 years vary broadly according to the situation and intention of the people involved. Examples include system design, strategic planning, product design, community development, resolution of environmental disputes, and many more. Despite the diversity of specific outcomes, there has also been a remarkable commonality of emergent behaviors, which I describe as follows: High Learning, High Play, Appropriate Structure and Control, Genuine Community, and Authentic Leadership.

High Learning

High Learning is a phrase borrowed in part from Thomas Kuhn[10] who wrote of High Science as being one of those paradigm busting moments of scientific insight. I have changed "science" to "learning" in recognition of the fact that not all of us do science,

---

10   Thomas Kuhn, *The Structures of Scientific Revolution* (University of Chicago Press, 1962).

but we all learn, and occasionally we learn with breathtaking speed
and clarity. In OST it is a common experience that previously
unthought of, and perhaps unthinkable, ideas show up with regularity, allowing impossible situations to find resolution when
apparently conflicting ideas coalesce to form novel approaches. In
retrospect the ideas and solutions may seem obvious and natural,
but in prospect they are so far out of the box as to be off the table
and out of mind.

High Play

One of the more curious aspects of all OST gatherings is the
presence of play. Even in the most serious of situations where
major conflict and complex issues dominate, there is a playful
atmosphere. Play, as I am using the word here, is not a trivial activity to be distinguished from "real work." Rather it is a manner of
being together characterized by an easy give and take, and the
presence of humor, even under the most dire circumstances. The
importance of play, particularly in situations where High Learning
is also taking place, lies in the interesting capacity of play to provide an antidote to premature closure and dogmatism.

When a new reality confronts us (a challenge, task, or set of
circumstances), there is necessity to make some sense out of it all.
Typically this sense-making is accomplished by offering an "explanation" which, more often than not, takes the form of a story or
theory, in which the available facts are assembled in some rational
way. Inevitably the early versions of this story are flawed simply
because all the facts are not known, or if known, then not fully
understood. If such an early version is taken to be "gospel truth,"
the results can be difficult and lead to a dogmatic foreclosure of

discussion. On the other hand if the new story, or theory, is created with a playful spirit there is as much enjoyment tearing it down as building it up. It is in this constructive/destructive process that a better story is made, or theory propounded.

Appropriate Structure and Control

An opinion common to those who either have just heard about OST, or who have only had the opportunity to briefly witness such an event without ever being an actual participant, is that there's little structure and no controls. Typically this refers to the fact that activities take place without overt direction (certainly by the facilitator) and the observable structure is loose at best, and constantly subject to change. Compared to what might be called a "standard meeting," this opinion has apparent validity. However, careful observation of any Open Space event will reveal a level of structure and control that is typically vastly in excess of that found in even the most tightly organized (planned) situations. For example, in one of the larger OST gatherings, 2108 German psychiatrists/psychologists gathered to explore and expand their field of endeavor. In the first hour of meeting they created 234 individual discussion groups which then met concurrently over the next 8 hours, ending with written reports from each of the sessions. The complex structure required to channel the energy of 2108 individuals, in and out of 234 working groups, with end products of written reports—is probably beyond the capacity of most conference planning/management groups to imagine, let alone design and implement. And yet this was all produced in less than an hour with sufficient controls to sustain operations and produce a product. But there is a significant difference—the structure and controls manifest in OST are *emergent,* which is to say that they emanate from the group as a whole and therefore are *appropriate* to the people involved, the task in front of them, and the environment in which everything is taking place. If any of these factors change (people, task, environment) both structure and controls will change virtually instantaneously.

Genuine Community

One of the most curious results of virtually every OST is the appearance of what I can only call Genuine Community. Even in the most conflicted and complex environments it is not uncommon to see sworn enemies engaging each other with respect, which then yields a degree of trust, and even hope. By the conclusion of the gathering, heartfelt hugs, even kisses may be exchanged—made all the more remarkable by the fact that zero effort had been expended in pursuit of such behavior. There had been no mediation, conflict resolution, or relationship building exercises. But somehow in a very warm, organic manner, authentic human relationships appear to blossom: Genuine Community. It is genuine in the sense that it was neither encouraged, or imposed as sometimes happens in the typical office party when an exuberant CEO proclaims that, "We are all one family." In OST, Community just happens.

Authentic Leadership

First time participants in an Open Space often find it very confusing because everything appears to be happening in an orderly, productive fashion and no one is in charge. At least no one is playing the expected role of The Leader. It is true that the event starts with some brief comments from the single facilitator (usually about 15 minutes), but the "instructions" are simple to the point of nonexistence. In fact they are hardly instructions, but rather an invitation to identify what each person genuinely cares about in terms of issues related to the business at hand, and then take responsibility for what they care about. After 15 minutes, the facilitator's role becomes little more than being a mobile microphone stand with larger groups, and with smaller numbers (no need for a microphone), the facilitator will simply sit down. The subsequent role of the facilitator is even less obvious, in fact I will often take a nap once things are under way. It is sort of a mantra amongst OST facilitators that we should be totally present and absolutely invisible. Clearly, if the facilitator is supposed to be The Leader, he or she is not doing the job.

And yet somehow orderly and purposeful work takes place. Issues are raised, groups are formed, useful discussion occurs, reports are written, and actions are initiated, all without benefit of The Leader, or indeed anybody—Taking Charge. If asked about this situation, participants will often reply with a quizzical tone saying, "There is no leadership." This is usually followed by a smile and words to the effect—Yes there is. We are all leaders.

It becomes apparent that while The Leader is totally absent, the function of Leadership is exercised in a most effective fashion. This function has been defined in multiple ways, but at the simplest level I suggest that *Leadership provides the stimulus, direction, and focus for useful activity*. That activity may be playing a game, designing a building, or running a business, but in all situations not much of utility will take place until a direction is established and attention is focused on the business at hand, and that is the primary function of Leadership. In every Open Space, that function is clearly exercised, but where does it come from, and how does it work?

I believe the genesis of Leadership comes from two sources: Passion and Responsibility. Or more precisely, Leadership emerges at the confluence of Passion and Responsibility. When individuals clearly identify what they truly care about (have passion for), and take personal responsibility for what is happening, things start to move. Passion alone may be flashy, but it may also be just a flash in the pan, all sizzle but no steak. Responsibility alone is simply boring. But passion united with responsibility create the needed sense of direction and focus that can get the job done. That is Leadership.

What may appear to be a theoretical statement is in fact the product of 20 years' observation in countless Open Space gatherings around the world. Participants are invited to identify issues they really care about (passion) and take responsibility for them, which in the first instance means that the participant will convene a dis-cussion group on that issue. And all those who care about the same issue are invited to attend. Of course, those who come may care about that issue in radically different ways, but the commonality of their caring is what brings them together. They organize, or more exactly self-organize, and thereby create what I call *a nexus of caring*.

A Nexus of Caring is analogous to (equivalent?) the Strange Attractor of Chaos and Complexity theory. Strange Attractors, we are told, create the hot spots of organization, drawing the disparate elements of the chaotic stew into a new and coherent alignment. This is the beginning of order, a new order more complex and (potentially) better able to cope with the environment. The Nexus of Caring performs exactly the same function in Open Space.

There is no guarantee that the group will come to a successful conclusion, but the probabilities are pretty good. When caring people gather around something they care about, there is a high likelihood that useful things will happen. But please note, it is the original appearance of passion and responsibility which sets the whole process in motion and provides the initial focus and direction for the group. This is Leadership doing what it does.

In large Open Spaces there will be literally hundreds of these Nexi of Caring. From moment to moment over the course of a day, the function of leadership will pass from person to person, and at any one point in time there will be multiple people assuming this role. Were one to map the passage of leadership it would be a dense and confusing map, to say the least. And clearly the old organizational chart, with its hierarchical format, is simply inadequate for the task. Most of all, The Leader is nowhere to be found.

What can be found is what I have called Authentic Leadership. It is authentic in the sense that it is emergent from the group itself, and totally congruent with the people involved, the task they have undertaken, and the environment in which they work. And should any of these elements change, Leadership will change virtually instantaneously. All of this contrasts starkly with the more traditional understanding of Leadership in which the One, or the few, are predesignated to command and control the many. From the viewpoint of such a traditional understanding, what happens in Open Space is curious at best, and probably outrageous, but it works—and continues to work in thousands of iterations of the Open Space experiment.

Peter Vaill's Behavioral Characteristics of High Performing Systems

The preceding list of behavioral characteristics of Open Space gatherings was developed during years of observation. They continue to reflect my perception of the results achieved by the natural experiment. However, I might equally have used the HPS Behavioral Characteristics described by Peter Vaill to accurately describe the situation, and they all seem to show up. Interesting coincidence or a substantial bridge toward a new(er) understanding of the quest for High Performance? The former is certainly possible, but I will argue for the latter.

The Hypothesis—First Take

Every good experiment must have an hypothesis which may be proved or negated. Ordinarily the hypothesis appears at the beginning of the experiment, but with a natural experiment the process is reversed, for it is usually the case that the experiment is well under way before it is clear that there exists a genuine question, an hypothesis worthy of testing. As you will understand, this was definitely the case with OST. So what is the hypothesis?

One possible version might go something like this: *Human beings in OST will perform at superior levels relative to their expectations and prior experience provided the experimental conditions are present and the procedure followed.* Given the global experience with OST, this hypothesis appears well on the way to validation. But all of that presumes that Open Space Technology is, in itself, the operative mechanism, and frankly, given the utter simplicity of the method, and the manner in which it was developed, that appears to me to be highly questionable.

How could something so simple do so much? What power, force, or mechanism lies behind, or beneath, Open Space? Why does Open Space Technology work anyhow? If we had some clues in this department we might develop a truly interesting hypothesis.

The Power Behind OST

With the conventional understanding of the management of meetings and organizations, there is precious little reason to expect that sitting in a circle, creating a bulletin board, and opening a marketplace could produce the results that have been experienced with Open Space Technology. At some fundamental level, OST is counterintuitive and basically wrong. It should not happen. It could not happen. But it does.

A clue to the resolution of this conundrum showed up for me in the early 90s. For some years I had been fascinated with the work of Ilya Prigogine, a chemist who had found strong evidence that order could appear out of chaos in a seemingly natural and inexorable manner without benefit of an external "organizer." This unorthodox, and perhaps even heretical finding grew out of work Prigogine[11] had done in the early 1970s and for which he received the Nobel Prize. Prigogine discovered that when otherwise stable chemicals were subject to some level of environmental change they moved into a far from equilibrium state (chaos). On the yonder side they would either fall apart, or become re-organized at new and higher levels of complexity, capable of dealing with the

---

11 Ilya Prigogine, *Order Out of Chaos* (Bantam Books, 1984).

changed environment. The curious thing is that they seemed to do this all by themselves, and virtually instantaneously. In a word: self–organization.

A visual image of this process, offered by Prigogine, is that of the teapot. Filled with water and placed on a cold stove, the water simply sits there in a placid, ordered state. But when the heat is turned on (environment changes) the water commences to move in a chaotic, random fashion. Little bubbles appear here and there on the surface in no apparent order, and the rate of appearance increases as the heat goes up until the whole body of water exists in a chaotic jumble. Then a most remarkable thing occurs. The random, chaotic bubbles convert, virtually instantaneously, into the ordered flow of a rolling boil. A new and higher order of complexity has been achieved commensurate with the changed environmental circumstances. And it happens all by itself.

The image of self–organization paralleled our growing experience with life in OST. A group of people would begin sitting quietly in a circle, but in short order that static state dissolved into a chaos of movement as issues were announced and posted on the wall. And all semblance of order disappeared when the entire group left their seats to approach the wall (marketplace) to negotiate time and place of meeting. However, as quickly as the chaos of the moment appeared it disappeared, now resolved into multiple smaller groups gathered in a new and more complex order to pursue the business at hand. The visual similarity was striking, but was it anything more than an interesting happenstance? After all, it is a long way from chemistry and teapots to the world of human organization.

A Closer Link—The Work of Stuart Kauffman

Stuart Kauffman is a biologist who has been closely associated with the Santa Fe Institute. Kauffman was fascinated with the origin of life and the interesting question of how it was that living things appeared out of the molecular stew bubbling on a young planet. Based upon a combination of computer modeling and laboratory research, Kauffman came to the startling conclusion that everything seemed to happen pretty much by itself. Or, as he says with mantra-like regularity in his book, *At Home in the Universe*[12]—"Order for free!"

More specifically, Kauffman found that given certain very simple preconditions, order happens. And not just any order, but highly complex order characteristic of living systems, which he calls Complex Adaptive Systems. They are *complex* in that they consist of multiple parts aggregated in myriad ways, *adaptive* in that they are constantly changing to meet the requirements of a shifting environment, and a *system* in that these parts not only fit together but do so in a purposeful fashion. In short they *do* something.

The essential preconditions,[13] according to Kauffman are as follows: (1) *A relatively safe, nutrient environment*, (2) *Diversity of elements*, (3) *Complexity of connection*, (4) *Search for fitness*, (5) *Sparse prior connections*, (6) *Being at the edge of chaos*.

(1)   *A relatively safe, nutrient environment*—The elements of the "to-be-organized system" must exist in relative safety. In terms of the

---

12 Stuart Kauffman, *At Home in the Universe* (Oxford University Press, 1995).

13 The "essential preconditions" listed here are in a sense a reconstruction of Kauffman's work in that he never actually lists them as I have here. I believe, however, that I have them basically correct.

early Earth, we might see all of this taking place behind a shel-
tering rock which provided shielding from the Sun's rays.

(2) *Diversity of elements*—If the molecular stew is homogeneous (all
the same thing), self-organization will not occur. Conversely,
the higher degree of diversity, the better the chances for self-
organization.

(3) *Complexity of connection*—If the available elements will only fit
together in a single way, the possibility for self-organization is
low. On the other hand, as the number and kinds of "atomic
hooks" increase, so also the probability that the odd atoms
and molecules will hitch up in a novel fashion, productive of
new order.

(4) *Search for fitness*—this precondition is essentially the core principle of Darwinian evolution which is often rendered, incorrectly
I believe, as the "survival of the fittest." The real point is that the
evolutionary process should be understood as a continuing
movement by all life forms toward a better "fit" within themselves (enhanced internal system function) and with their environment. It also turns out that those who fit best, survive best,
but this is not so much a competitive process as an adaptive
one. At the end of the day most truly successful species achieve
that success not so much through the elimination of competitors, but rather by learning effective collaboration. True symbio-
sis, it appears, is infinitely more effective than outright war.
Kauffman suggests that a similar process occurs with the various atoms and simple molecules coalescing to form the hugely
complex molecules of life. Admittedly, "searching for fitness" at
the atomic and molecular level implies a degree of conscious

intent on the part of these wee critters. But conscious or not, it seems that the search goes on. At least Kauffman thinks it does.

(5) *Sparse prior connections*—This one is actually less esoteric than it sounds. The point is simply that self-organization is difficult when everything is already organized, and all the connections made. Hence, sparse prior connections.

(6) *On the edge of chaos*—The final precondition is probably the critical one. All of the preceding conditions might be present, but if the "to-be-organized" material is just sitting like an inert blob, nothing much will happen. On the other hand if it is a boiling caldron of random stew—look out. Self-organization is on the way.

The Open Space Connection

The connection between Open Space Technology and Kauffman's preconditions may be tenuous or solid, but when reading Kauffman the similarity between what Kauffman described, and what I identified as the essential conditions for OST (see above), definitely caught my attention. The correlation at a verbal level was obvious, particularly with reference to *complexity* and *diversity*, but it seemed to go a lot further. For example, my observations that OST worked best when there was a real business issue in need of resolution and a decision time of yesterday (real urgency) sounded very much like *Searching for fitness* but with a vengeance. And when it came to *Being at the edge of chaos*, that was, in my judgment a perfect match for OS condition #4—*High levels of passion and (potential) conflict*. Even if the words did not match, the actual experience certainly seemed to. At the beginning of what I might call a "really juicy" OST, feelings are definitely high and the possibility of predicting outcomes is remote. Chaos is not an inappropriate word for the situation.

One of Kauffman's preconditions did present something of a challenge: *Sparse prior connections.* The problem lay in the fact that, if this precondition also applied to OST then it would appear that highly bureaucratic organizations—where everything is connected—would not do well in OST. But the experience had been quite the opposite. In fact I had never been able to perceive any basic difference in function between loosely (or recently) organized groups and those with a long history of rigid structure. If all other OS conditions were in place, the performance/process was the same. How come?

After reflection, it occurred to me that the secret probably lay with the circle and the way that every OST begins (with everybody sitting in a circle). Over the course of human history, the circle, and its powers, has been an area of constant interest, but setting aside the more esoteric possibilities, it seemed to me that the clue lay in the very practical and mechanical function of the circle in OST. At the start, there is simply a circle of chairs, with no seating assignments. People sit where they choose and/or where space is available. Hence their actual position in the circle is attributable to individual whim or time of arrival, and the group, no matter what its history, is effectively "randomized." The net effect is that prior connections, at least in terms of sitting patterns, are disaggregated.

The Bottom Line

I make bold to suggest that what Kauffman has described and what we have witnessed in OST are the same, or certainly comparable. And if one is to search for the fundamental operating mechanism which makes Open Space Technology possible, even when it seems counterintuitive and wrong, that mechanism is quite simply the power of self-organization. I recognize that the world of atoms and molecules is rather different than the world of human groups, and that I could well be straining the coherence of Kauffman's science by making such a connection. And since Kauffman's science is, in itself, a matter of some continuing debate,[14] my conclusion could be fatuous, and founded on a bed of quicksand. That said, I know of no other theoretical framework which enables useful sense making out of the 20 year experience in OST.

Open Space as Self-Organization

When OST is viewed as an example of self-organization in action, many mysteries appear to resolve, particularly if it is remembered that self-organization is fundamental to all of life and the cosmos as a whole. In short it is a force with a very long history, predating all such modern inventions as group work, facilitation, large group interventions, and the like. Open Space Technology works simply and only because the essential preconditions for self-organization were serendipitously identified and brought into play under the influence of two martinis. Viewed from the position of the standard understanding of meeting and organization, what happens in OST is impossible. Seen as self-organization, the interesting occurrences which take place in all Open Space gatherings are predictable.

So for example, if one were to wonder how a large group of people could move from a state of passivity, with no precise idea of where they were going, or how they were going to get there, into a state of productive involvement with only a 15-minute talk as their

---

14 I must leave the final judgment of Kauffman's work to his peers and colleagues, but I would note in this regard that my reading of the responsible scientific critique of his work suggests that many would now agree that he is definitely onto something, even if all the details have yet to be worked out.

guide—the answer is they already "knew." That "knowledge" had been essentially hardwired into their collective mentality and had been there for millennia.

Or another mystery. How could it be that OST seemingly works everywhere on the globe regardless of culture, religion, ethnicity, economics, education, or any of the other supposedly important variables of the human race? Even more curious, it seems to work in exactly the same way, to the point that the behaviors manifest (what I have called the "experimental results") are identical in all places. To be sure there are differences in terms of language, dress, and the issues under discussion, but at a broader level it is absolutely true: If you have seen one OST, you have seen them all. And how could this be? The answer: The operative mechanism is essentially prior to all such variables. Before culture, before religion, before economics and education—self-organization was.

And should you ask—is all of this true, my response can only be, I think so. At the very least it is a workable hypothesis subject to testing anywhere, anytime you choose to run the experiment. That said, I would add that resolving the mysteries of Open Space Technology is perhaps the least important consequence of the connection between OST and self-organization. Infinitely more important would be a deeper understanding of the nature of High Performance (Systems) and how we might achieve it on some regular basis.

Open Space, Self-Organization, and High Performance

The logic here is simple and straightforward. If High Performance shows up with regularity in OST, and OST itself is a product of self-organization, then it would appear reasonable that High Performance (Systems) has its source in the power of Self-Organization. Directly stated: *Self-organization drives inexorably toward High Performance which is the realization of the Search for Fitness.* This goal may or may not be achieved, but when it is—there is a manifest fitness internally and externally. Internally the myriad organizational functions and elements work smoothly together, and externally the organization exists in a fully symbiotic relationship with the environment. And it happens all by itself.

Should the logic offered above accord with reality, the attainment of High Performance is less a matter of doing something (as in designing, installing, and maintaining the pieces of organizational life) but rather—*being* fully and intentionally what we already are—a self-organizing system. Or, in the central image of this book, become a Wave Rider surfing this powerful force in our world.

At a more practical level, the multiple obstacles to the achievement of High Performance considered in our opening chapters are substantially mitigated, if not removed. As long as the creation of a truly High Performing System depends upon our capacity to "find the problem and fix it," thereby leaving us to the mercy of unintended consequences, we will find ourselves in the predicament of the ancient Greek king, Sisyphus. As quickly as we push the rock of organization dysfunction up the hill toward resolution it returns with greater force accompanied by a whole new set of unforeseen problems. Even if we apply the latest insights of systemic thinking, our efforts at self-help see little improvement. Indeed, our situation substantially deteriorates. We now know, in agonizing detail, the mind-boggling complexity and connectivity of that apparently simple thing called "Our Business." Perhaps some day we may reach the end of the tunnel and discover that errant butterfly flapping its wings thereby throwing our lives into chaos. But I wouldn't hold my breath. Going the way we are going we will never find the Holy Grail—High Performance Systems. Humpty Dumpty will remain in pieces, and although we may name them all (except for the infinite number of pieces yet to be found), the puzzle will remain unsolved and unsolvable.

But the good news is that we really do not have to take this trip. It may be academically interesting and intellectually challenging (all good things) but there is a better way to our goal. The power of self-organization thrives on an infinity of chaos and complexity—out of which order and high performance appear. And it happens all by itself. Furthermore it has been happening for 13.7 billion years.

The Hypothesis—Second Take

The leap from a 2–3 day Open Space event into the realm of "all human systems" is monstrous. After all, an Open Space gathering is of relatively small size and short duration. And even if it were to be conclusively proved that self-organization were the operative power of OST and truly productive of High Performance, what relevance could this finding have for infinitely larger systems? The pursuit of this question requires a radical restatement of our hypothesis, which may now be rendered as follows: *All human systems are self-organizing and naturally tend toward high performance provided the essential preconditions are present and sustained.*

The assertion that all human systems are self-organizing is probably unprovable in any absolute sense, and is definitely unorthodox when viewed against the more conventional view that our organizations are our creatures. We did the organizing, and if not us, then somebody. Surely such institutions as General Motors, the U.S. Federal Government, to say nothing of Wal–Mart and the Red Cross, appeared through careful design, and reappeared through multiple re–organizations, all conducted by us. The hypothesis starts from a different place. All systems from beginning to end, top to bottom, start to finish—are self–organizing. In a word, *there is no such thing as a non–self-organizing system.*

The additional assertion that such systems are naturally productive of high performance, provided the essential preconditions are present is, at least comparatively, less revolutionary. In fact, it is almost a tautology. If Kauffman is correct that Complex Adaptive Systems are constantly searching for a better way to be within themselves and their environment, increasing levels of performance would be a natural outcome. This would not require that such organizations be superstars on a global scale, only that they do better than average in their own context. Small fish in small ponds can also be outstanding.

Chapter VI

Self-Organization: The Key to High Performance Systems?

The jump from the very limited situation of an Open Space event into the infinitely larger realm of human systems of all sizes is considerable, to say the least. However it is not without precedent. Making such a move is, in fact, the common practice of "scaling up." When some new product demonstrates its effectiveness in the experimental environment, the next step is to shift from the "micro" to the "macro." There is no guarantee of success, but the decision to move onward is easier when it appears that similar conditions pertain at both levels. In this particular situation the critical question is—what likelihood exists that large human systems are fundamentally self-organizing? In the event that Open Space Technology represents only a special, limited case, all reasons to move up the food chain simply disappear. On the other hand, were we to have some reasonable expectation of similar conditions at the macro level, making the move becomes much more attractive.

Arrayed against the feasibility of such a journey is the solid tradition of the conventional wisdom, buttressed by decades of theory and practice in Management Science. Organizations come into being when they are organized, and we all know who did that—us. Or if not us, then somebody. To suggest otherwise is unthinkable. Or is it?

Let's suppose that Stuart Kauffman, Ilya Prigogine, along with their countless peers and colleagues in the sciences, are correct in proposing that self-organization is a fundamental mechanism behind the origin and development of the cosmos. Including, of course, that small and lately arrived aspect of the cosmos known as life, and more particularly, human life. Self-organization would then take its place alongside the other primal forces, such as gravity, in the order of things. Under these circumstances it would be just as likely that human systems escape the dominion of self-organization as that they might operate free from gravity. A theoretical possibility for sure, but rather unlikely.

On the other hand we all know how our businesses and organizations came into being. They were designed, carefully or poorly, by some human beings. We even have pictures to prove it; first and foremost the omnipresent Organization Chart. On a single piece of paper, or often in a whole book, the finely wrought, carefully planned description of how everything works is offered for our reflection and guidance. And to suggest that this paragon of organization was the work of some fatuous force makes as much sense as the proposition that a group of monkeys, banging randomly on typewriters, could eventually produce Shakespeare.

However, that famous organization chart may be something less than meets the eye. At least that has always been my experience when beginning a new assignment with a client. As a matter of courtesy and for my education, I am presented with the official document upon arrival, shortly followed by the caveat that it is out of date, and not to be trusted. Here is the mother lode of organization, the product of infinite hours of dedicated work—and it can't be trusted. Then, if you were to ask, as I often did—how you actually got things done around the place, the answer would ordinarily come back in terms of what I call the Lucy Syndrome. When you need something done, go and see Lucy.

Lucy and the Informal Organization

As it turns out, Lucy (or some similar person with a different name) was a clerk in Accounting. She was so far off the Organization Chart as to be invisible, however, she had been with the organization for 20 years and knew everybody, if only because she passed out the paychecks. If Lucy didn't know what to do, or who to talk to, you might as well give up right there. In addition to passing out the paychecks, Lucy also spent considerable time on the phone and at the watercooler. Some might call it gossip, but the cognoscenti knew that Lucy sat at the crossroads of that wonderful thing called the Informal Organization. If it happened, could have happened, didn't happen, or might have happened—Lucy knew about it before anybody. And as we all know, knowledge is power. To be sure, Lucy was a little hazy about some of the technical details, but in the case of need, she knew exactly who to talk to.

Lucy also had her favorites, that special group of people, young and old, with whom she took special pains to "keep in the loop." And of course it was a two-way street, for what she gave, she also received in abundance. Induction into Lucy's Loop was a matter of pride and real power. If nothing else "membership" separated the Newbies (new hires) from the old hands. The Newbies frantically search the Organization Chart and the accompanying Manual of Procedures, seeking some clue as to how the place worked. The old hands just get on with the business.

The power of the Informal Organization is a well kept secret, in part because the keepers of the formal system, otherwise known as The Managers, have dedicated themselves to the abolition of the informal system. At some level it is their job. Everything should be done in a formal, orderly way, by the book as it were—beginning with formal communications and formal procedures. The Informal Organization is, of course, the antithesis of all of that, and its appearance an obvious threat to management and The Management. Better out of sight and out of mind, lest job performance be questioned.

The Informal Organization fares no better in the organizational literature. If mentioned at all, it is usually consigned to a footnote or a little side comment. Case in point is the work of Gary Dressler in his book, *Management: Leading People and Organizations in the 21st Century*.[15] He writes, "The informal organization, which does not appear on any organizational chart, consists of the informal contacts among themselves that employees use to get the job done." As near as I can tell, this is just about all he has to say on the subject. This seems a little odd since he understands the informal system to be a critical element which "employees use to get the job done."

Despite the best efforts of Management, the Informal Organization is alive and well. And were you to ask who created this organization, the answer would be universally clear—nobody. It happened pretty much all by itself. One might say, self-organization.

---

15 Gary Dressler, *Management: Leading People and Organizations in the 21st Century*, 2nd edition (Prentice Hall, 2000, p. 212).

What Good Is the Informal Organization?

We may take it as a given that the Informal Organization has existed within organizations forever. But the simple fact of prevalence does not make it either good or useful. Hence the question: What good is the Informal Organization?

According to the opinion of many managers, the informal system is the complete antithesis of what every good organization should be. And yet if you listen carefully to these same people, the diabolical nature of the informal system is less than clear. This is particularly true in off the record discussions, usually over a drink or in other casual situations, when the conversation turns to "how things *really* get done." At that point all the "war stories" come out. The story behind the story of some major corporate breakthrough never seems to accord with the official version.

A startling, new technological invention, the star in the corporate crown, often sees the first light of day, if only as an idea, under rather questionable circumstances. The stories are various, but will often take a common pattern such as the research team had a really hard day. Nothing seemed to go right and progress was measured in minus quantities. There seemed little to do but hang up the towel and adjourn to the local watering hole for some attitude adjustment. After the first drink, the atmosphere lightened and the banter began. The bar person made some off the wall comment, and a junior associate answered in kind—pure trivial conversation and certainly never to be confused with high science. However, further down the bar another team member suddenly felt the odd sensation of a light going on. Somehow related to the conversation at hand, but not in a way that anybody could trace—the niggling budding of a half-formed idea took shape in his mind. Suddenly bar napkins and coasters became the tools of science and scrawled equations, written in haste, were passed up and down. After several hours of excited conversation, the party was over. Napkins and coasters were gathered and stuffed into a pocket to await the morning.

Far be it from me to ascribe all scientific inventions to the bar-room environment, but I would be greatly surprised if they all happened the way they "were supposed to." The funny story of Post-its, told often as an odd, anomalous happening, is probably pretty close to the rule. The reason we don't hear about more examples has a lot to do, I think, with the public image of those involved. After all, how many distinguished scientists would like it to be generally known that their prize winning creation had its beginnings in a bar? And certainly by the time corporate blessing and future funding are being sought, all traces of the true genesis have been scrubbed. Lists of experts consulted, journals read, and experiments conducted, now constitute the official record. But those in Lucy's Loop, who have heard the story, know differently.

So what good is the informal organization? It may well be the critical seed bed of innovation, the source of novelty—even very small and apparently insignificant novelties. The formal system seemingly does quite well with "business as usual," but when difference and deviation are the norm, the performance is less than gratifying. To the uncritical eye it may well appear that the vast majority of situations fall easily under the heading of Business as Usual. But every skilled craftsman and technician knows that each situation is unique, requiring a little twist or turn, an odd piece of knowledge that never quite made it into the formal system enshrined in the Standard Book of Procedure. For the old hands (read "experienced") the coffeepot and the watercooler are the fonts of such useful knowledge, for that is where the Informal System flows and Lucy reigns.

Working to Rule

But surely, I must be exaggerating. For all the effort that has been devoted to the organization and re-organization of the formal systems of our world, there must be a better payoff. I believe there is a payoff of considerable utility, but probably not of the sort we intended. If it was our expectation to make things work better through the tight formalization of processes and procedures, the heart and soul of the Formal Organization—then I think we have missed the boat. However, there are definite, albeit more limited, benefits which we will consider in a moment, but first a closer look at the "workability" of the Formal Organization. It is all about *Working to Rule*.

Working to Rule refers to a practice adopted in many union shops when it is necessary to bring recalcitrant management to the table for a discussion. The tactic is the exact opposite of a strike in which all work ceases. In fact work continues, but in a manner precisely described by the rules of the current contract. Everything that is required or prohibited is done/not done *exactly* as the contract specifies. One might think that such an approach would be applauded by management, if only because the formal system is observed in exquisite detail. The actual impact is rather different.

When each element of the contract is followed to the letter of the law, useful work slows, and in some cases ceases all together. I think there is a lesson here: *If we actually did business the way we say we do business, we would go out of business.* This statement may be a bit of an *over*statement, but it points I believe, to the limitations, nature, and function of the Formal System.

The Nature and Function of the Formal System

Formal System here refers to what we actually create or organize, which for the most part shows up on a printed page or a computer screen. With endless patience and fine detail (in the best of situations), we create designs indicating what we think should happen, hope will happen, or expect to happen. In words and charts we describe the organization as we understand it, and indicate the desired behaviors. There is no doubt that we do the creating, and the awesome power of self-organization definitely takes a back seat. However, there comes that wonderful moment when our carefully crafted designs are implemented. And suddenly the closed systems of our minds become open as they are thrown into the complex and ever-changing world of our experience. In a word, our designs become simply one more element in the ongoing process of self-organization. With that passage the rules change. Whatever internal mechanisms we may have designed into our system are now re-contexted and outflanked by the principles and functions of self-organization. The situation might be analogous to that faced by some future astronaut who had spent the majority of his life out in space, living under the conditions of weightlessness.

On the space station, processes and procedures were created, and they worked flawlessly. But on the return to Earth, and gravity, a whole mess of stuff went clunk! The rules had changed.

Admittedly this view is at some variance with present understanding and practice. While there is a growing recognition of the real presence of self-organization, that recognition appears, at best, to be grudging. The formal system (what we organized) and the self-organizing system (what happened all by itself) are taken to be parallel systems, with the formal system in a position of dominance. My view is radically different. As I said, there is no such thing as a non–self-organizing system. Even something as carefully drawn as a sophisticated accounting system becomes self-organizing at the moment of implementation. The same could be said for a software system. As long as it is in the box, the software stands in splendid isolation. But the moment the first user shows up, the rules have changed.

That said, I do believe our formal systems have great utility, albeit with limits. And it is most important to understand what the utility and limits may be. *Fundamentally, our formal systems are maps which describe the territory in which we do business.* These maps may be very carefully drawn and based upon an infinite amount of experience—but at the end of the day, they are still maps. Organizational Charts map the relationships and functions of the people involved. Strategic Plans map these relationships and functions over time, indicating our expectations and hopes for the future. However, as Alfred Korzybski points out, "A map *is not* (italics mine) the territory."[16] And to

---

16 Alfred Korzybski, *Science and Sanity: An Introduction to non-Aristotelian Systems and Semantics*, 5th Edition (Institute of General Semantics, 1994, p. 58).

confuse the map with the territory is to invite dysfunction at the least, and total disaster in many circumstances. Organization Charts do not create the organization. Strategic Plans do not create the future for the organization. Both charts and plans simply (and only) express our best guess/hope/expectation regarding organizational function over time.

Doubtless there are precious few senior managers or executives who would disagree in principle with what I have said. However, I believe it to be true that regardless of the degree of agreement at the level of theory, in practice many (and perhaps most) organizations continue to operate *as if* the formal organization were dominant, or indeed the only thing. Not all that long ago the definition of a "good manager" went as follows: "A good manager makes the plan, manages to the plan, and meets the plan." The power of this definition may be a little tenuous these days, but the desire to make the plan and meet the numbers continues in full force.

Granted the limitations—what is the utility of the Formal System? The utility is the same as with any map, and the better the map, the more useful. But it is particularly useful for outsiders and newcomers. For outsiders, the organizational maps provide a rough idea of the general shape and points of contact. Banks, for example, need to know who has authority to sign checks, and customers need to know where to complain in the event of dissatisfaction. Investors need to know the intended future direction and current conditions of the institution. The organization chart and the strategic plan provide that information. However, a serious investor understands that due diligence has not been performed with a review of the maps. Even a very careful review will not tell it all, but it is certainly a place to start.

The second population, which finds the maps particularly helpful, are the newcomers. New hires require points of orientation as
they make their way in the strange environment—at least until
they meet Lucy and her associates.

In a word, the organizational maps are of great utility in *the
boundary situations.* At the organizational edges, customers, bankers,
and other outsiders need to know where to go for information and
services. For newcomers, the organizational maps perform an
analogous function, helping them cross the boundaries, and point-
ing them in the direction of the essential resources required for the
performance of their jobs. These "essential resources" are, for the
most part, particular people, whose names appear on the Organization Chart, and known collectively as the Formal Leadership.

Formal Leadership

When thinking of the Formal Leadership it is most important to
remember one of the critical results from the Open Space
Experiment, which I referred to as Authentic Leadership. We found
that in Open Space the function of Leadership manifests at the
junction of passion and responsibility. Further, that this function
may be exercised by virtually anyone, passing from individual
to individual as the needs of the people, their task, and the
environmental conditions change. I believe that the finding from
Open Space applies generally across the broader world of all
self-organizing systems. In a word, Authentic Leadership is not a
matter of title and position, nor can it be predetermined. The
Formal Leadership of an organization is always a matter of title
and position, and it is definitely predetermined.

I confess to a degree of discomfort with the juxtaposition of Formal Leadership and Authentic Leadership, which might suggest that those who constitute the Formal Leadership are incapable of truly leading. That is not my intent, for in fact we have all known many individuals in the Formal Leadership who definitely exercise Authentic Leadership, and with distinction. Their passion and their sense of responsibility provide focus and direction as well as opening enormous amounts of space in which great things happen. Their capacity to exercise Authentic Leadership, however, is not a function of their title or position. That capacity comes from their unique passion and responsibility which created genuine Nexus of Caring. Of equal importance, these individuals were always willing to step aside when some creative, new Nexus of Caring puts in an appearance. Indeed they will applaud such an appearance. One would hope, therefore, that those individuals constituting the Formal Leadership will manifest Authentic Leadership, and in fact they often do—which in itself is sufficient reason to give them the title and position. And should the time come when they rarely if ever manifest such qualities of leadership, that will be the time for their removal. In between times, their position in the Formal Organization constitutes an essential point of contact in boundary situations, a critical part of the organizational map.

Organizational Maps as Points of Reference

Organizational maps have an additional function to provide checkpoints along the way toward the future, which facilitates a comparison of present and past experience. It is in the perception of differential between the past and present that much real learning takes place. Of special note are those instances where the maps are total-ly vacant, or of equal importance, have it all wrong. The interpreta-tion of the perceived difference will obviously vary. Perhaps the previous observations were less than accurate—or perhaps some-thing really has changed? But no matter the interpretation, always remember that the maps are, by definition, at least one step behind the present moment. To presume the innate correctness of the map will, at the very least, limit the possibility of learning—and may lead to serious difficulty.

In sum, the Formal Organization (structure, procedures, rule books, etc.) is useful in all boundary situations, and as an aid to our learning. However it remains a map and not the territory, an adjunct but not the real show. When we forget this, for whatever reason, our effective level of function can only decline. And were we to make the ultimate error of presuming that the Formal Organization *was* The Organization, not only would we have the cart before the horse, I think we may well have run off the road. Off road we will find ourselves tangled in a thicket of rules and procedures, structures, and controls which can easily take on a life of their own to the point that we spend more time running the business than doing (the) business. That said, the Formal Organization is very useful, provided it supports and assists "real life." No more, no less.

All of which leads to a critical question: *What is the minimal level of formal organization necessary for effective organizational function?*—all considered under the rubric of "Think of one more thing *not* to do." Should it turn out that much of what we have created in the area of "formality" can and does happen pretty much by itself, we could save considerable time and effort by eliminating unneeded tasks.

We will return to the question and the rubric in Part II of this book where we consider the practical details of our role as Wave Riders. For the moment, however, there is more ground to be covered as we assess the feasibility of scaling up from the Open Space Experiment into the infinitely larger world of real live organizations—particularly big ones.

Self-Organization in Really Big Systems

Presuming that I have not stretched my credibility to the breaking point, and that you have been able to follow my story, if only as a thought experiment, surely the next step could be the straw that breaks the camel's back. It is all very well to see the fine hand of self-organization operating in the small groups and back corridors of our businesses and institutions, but when it comes to the whole enchilada—surely I must be jesting. How on earth could thousands, worse yet hundreds of thousands, of people accomplish anything useful if left to the ultimate laissez faire of self-organization? At such a scale, the notion that the complex order required for productive human activity happened, "all by itself" is obviously absurd. Perhaps, but consider the following exercise which I have occasionally inflicted upon unsuspecting MBA students.

When the students have gathered, I congratulate them on their prowess in such areas as Systemic Thinking, Systems Design, and the like—noting that they have doubtless read all the relevant literature and are surely ready to put their skills to the test. That said, I offer the following exercise: Please design a system that will feed 8.5 million people everyday, anything they want, and always have two weeks' food supply on hand. Go!

When I see that they are really into their task and showing some real level of agitation (either because they think they have the solution or know that it is impossible), I put my hand in the air signaling a momentary pause. With a smile I say—"Sorry to say this, but this was all sort of a joke. You really don't have to design such a system. It already exists. It is called New York City. The reactions vary from outrage to passive acceptance, but the learning, generally speaking, is profound.

The feeding system of New York (or you could substitute any large city) is hugely complex and massive in scope. It is also largely effective in that most people eat quite well most of the time. For sure there are glitches and loopholes, but on any given day 8.5 million people get three meals from a cuisine of their choosing. And while most people can't see it, the larders of New York have two weeks' food supply on hand. Impressive—but even more impressive is the fact that absolutely nobody organized all of this. It happened all by itself. To be sure some people may have tried, and certainly there are groups that seek to influence the system such as the Public Health Department and the food pundits from the press—but in terms of overall system design and control— nothing, nada, zilch.

Now it might occur to you that were we to have a Culinary Executive Committee, with a proper planning department and CEO, the present situation could be infinitely improved. However, on the basis of strong historical evidence I submit that such an approach would be doomed from the start. In fact the approach has already been tried with disappointing results. In the closing years of the Soviet Union, where the practice of a managed economy extended to virtually all areas of life including the "feeding system," getting a good meal, well served was more than difficult unless you had outstanding luck or strong political connections. And by the end of the Soviet Union, getting any meal at all was sometimes quite difficult. Given a choice between dining out on the town in New York or Moscow, there was no choice.

It may concern you that the feeding system of New York is less than perfect. It is true that you can find hunger on the streets, and it is also true that no self-organizing system is perfect in some ideal sense. However the system is trying, which is what "adaptive" and "searching for fitness" are all about. But could you really call NYC "high performing"? Within the limits of our definition, I think the answer is yes. For all of its problems and imperfections, Gotham City certainly does better than the competition—in this case Moscow.

Proof or Probability?

Have we now proved that all systems, including very large systems, are self-organizing? Obviously not, but proof was never the intention. The objective was limited to raising the level of probability that large human systems, such as businesses, governments, and the like, were on the same planet with all the rest of us, and therefore subject to the same laws and powers. To this end we described the formal (clearly humanly organized) system in terms which more accurately depict what it actually is—a very useful map, but never to be confused with the territory. Simultaneously, we have attempted to release the informal system from the closet where it had long been held in disrepute. We also noted that when we actually do what the formal system requires in minute detail, the result most often is that useful work slows and even stops. And last but by no means least, we took a quick look at one of the largest systems that any of us are likely to encounter on a regular basis: the feeding system of New York City, or any other large metropolitan area. If anybody planned and organized it, they have yet to be identified, but somehow, and in spite of obvious imperfections, 8.5 million people manage to have their bellies filled on a regular basis. Some might call this a major miracle, but I believe self-organization will do.

If you are in agreement with the proposition that self-organization is the *likely* culprit underlying the genesis and motive power of our systems and are intrigued, if not persuaded, by the results of the 20-year natural experiment with Open Space Technology, we are approaching the point where we might proceed to the very practical considerations of our role as Wave Riders. But two further, and frankly painful, questions require our attention. First, if essential aspects of the process of self-organization include such unpleasantries as chaos, confusion, and conflict, to say nothing of ending and death—how do we deal with the pain? Second, if High Performance is the natural outcome of self-organization, and therefore happens pretty much by itself, why are we in such a mess?

Chapter **VII**

How Do We Deal with the Pain?

I have argued that true high performance, of the sort that Peter Vaill described, is the natural product of a well-functioning, self-organizing system. It comes ultimately from the search for fitness as the system seeks better ways to be—internally with its own mechanisms and processes, and externally with the relationships to the environment. This is an ongoing process of adaptation as changes, large and small, ripple inward and outward, initiating still more changes. Under the best of circumstances, the ongoing process is a complex symphony of movement productive of wholeness, health, and harmony—always in some degree of disequilibrium, on the way to something new. When the process ceases, the system ceases (dies)—but in the interim between start and finish, the search for fitness continues, marked on occasion by stunning insights and radical breakthroughs. But there is a cost. As the process of self-organization works its way, the powerful forces of chaos and confusion do their work—opening new space for novel approaches even as conflict smoothes, sharpens, and refines the outcomes. All are necessary and integral to the full life of a truly high performing self-organizing system, but none of them are free from pain. And how do we deal with the pain, particularly the pain of ending, as old, familiar patterns of life disappear?

There is a way, and it is called Griefwork. As old as humanity itself, it is seemingly hardwired into our psyches—and for sure it is not the modern invention of psychologists, psychotherapists, or grief counselors.The initial discovery and description of Griefwork may be credited to Elisabeth Kübler-Ross[17] whose seminal book brought death and grief out of the closet and helped us to understand the essential mechanisms in play as we deal with the approach of our own death, or the death of a loved one. My own work in this area led me to understand that the Griefwork process is operational not only at the level of the individual, but also the organization.[18] It appears to kick in whenever some significant aspect of our lives terminates, or is close to termination. In a word, Griefwork is available 24×7 for all of those moments when chaos, confusion, and conflict do their essential work, thereby enabling our self-organizing systems (us and our organizations) to negotiate the path toward high performance. The process of griefwork is not without pain, but it does lead us inexorably from a moment of ending to the dawn of renewal. We need only to follow.

It may appear to some that the introduction of Griefwork represents a disconnect from our discussion of the process of self-organization and high performance in human systems. But it is my belief that Griefwork is integral to the process, and essential for its full function in the realm of human systems. In a word,

---

17   Elisabeth Kübler-Ross, *On Death and Dying* (Collier Book, 1969).

18   Harrison Owen, *Spirit: Transformation and Development in Organizations* (Abbott Publishing, 1987, p. 104ff). Those familiar with the work of Kübler-Ross will notice that I have changed some of the terms and added some phases. These changes reflect my own observations of individuals and organizations, in addition to my personal experience of Griefwork.

Griefwork represents the natural adaptation of the human system, individually and collectively, to the conditions of self-organization. The initiating factor for this adaptation is the knowledge/remembrance of pain and death.

In other realms (atoms, molecules, stars, and "lower life forms"), as self-organization does its work, the forces of chaos, confusion, and conflict are fully operational. And it is also true that things come and go—they end and/or die. What is different in the human realm is consciousness. We remember the pain, and we know we are going to die.[19]

The remembrance of pain and the knowledge of death can have an adverse effect on the process of self-organization and the progress of (human) evolution. The simple fact of the matter is, we all go to great lengths to avoid both pain and death. Understandable, but also very costly in terms of our own evolution, and the possibility of achieving higher levels of performance. The usual (and rather muted) term for this is *risk avoidance*. In practice we make great effort to stay in protected places and known territory. As understandable as all this may be, it also has the undesirable consequence of stalling the process and essentially keeping us from exploring new possibilities. Were we somehow able to reconfigure the process to eliminate chaos, confusion, conflict, ending, and death—we might pass pain free into an eternity of evolution. Nice idea, but not too likely, I think. The alternative is to create effective

---

19 Whether and to what extent consciousness extends to all levels of the cosmos is a discussion I intend to avoid. It is apparent that animals remember pain and some (higher primates) appear to grieve. Whether this represents "consciousness" I leave for somebody else to determine. However, I do remember my pain and I know that I will die. And as near as I can determine, all my fellow *Homo sapiens* are in the same boat.

means of processing pain and death, and this is exactly what Griefwork accomplishes.

Griefwork might be compared with the human plumbing system, with which it shares certain similarities of function. It is the job of the human excretory system to safely remove the toxic by-products of life, the spent fuel of daily living. Griefwork performs the same function for our mental and emotional lives. Mentally we form stories and theories to explain the happenings of our world. To the extent that they are truly explanatory, we become very attached to them. Then the day comes when the world changes one more time. Everything we thought we knew and understood comes out wrong—and Griefwork commences. It may not be pleasant, but at the end we typically come up with some better story or theory.

A very similar thing happens with our emotional attachments, particularly when those attachments connect us to a fellow human being. The ending of a relationship, even a short-term relationship, is inevitably traumatic. But for most of us, most of the time, loves lost simply open the way for greater and deeper loves in our future. And Griefwork gets us there.

With apologies for the possible indelicacy of expression— Griefwork flushes our system, removing the bits and pieces of out-worn ideas and failed relationships, thereby clearing the decks for our future. It is Griefwork that ensures the continuing health of our enterprise by eliminating the toxins of organizational and personal life. As I said previously, High Performing Systems cannot be main-tained at the cost of a fouled nest, and Griefwork cleans up the nest. Like our plumbing system, it usually works all by itself with no conscious assistance.

The Griefwork Process

The Griefwork process goes into operation in the moment of ending, or the threat of ending. The "ending" in question may be ultimate, as in the ending of our life, the life of some organization with
which we are associated, or something less dramatic, such as the
termination of a favored theory, idea, project, or product. At the
moment of ending, or even the threat of ending, Griefwork starts.
Its initiation is totally automatic, and the progress of the stages
foreordained. In a word, it works pretty much all by itself. We did-
n't invent it, and certainly don't control it—but with increased
knowledge of what it is and how it works, we can assist ourselves
and our fellows through the process.

Shock and Anger

When the end comes, or is clearly on the horizon, the first
stage of Griefwork commences. Like an autonomic response in the
body, the process takes over without a thought. It appears as *Shock
and Anger.*

The individual expressions of Shock and Anger are as various
as the people on this earth, but at a verbal level they commonly
appear as two words. In English those words are "Oh shit!" Please
notice that "Oh golly" won't do. "Oh darn" just doesn't make it. But
"Oh shit," said with vigor, somehow says it all—lots of shock and
lots of anger.

Upon first hearing such an outburst, particularly if you are not
intimately involved in the ending/death, it may seem quite inappropriate. In fact, a normal reaction of those sitting on the sidelines
is to attempt some calming strategies combined with pleas for bet-

ter behavior. This is an error, for the words uttered are not simply profane but actually therapeutic.

The impact of the first stage of Griefwork is more physiological than psychological, for the immediate problem encountered by those in severe stress is physical shock, a condition in which bodily functions, particularly breathing, tend to become erratic. The common expression is that "It took my breath away." Shoulders hunch together, the chest is restricted, and taking a full breath is accomplished only as a painful act of will. And when you stop breathing, or breathe poorly, the prognosis is far from bright. However, all of that is quickly and automatically reversed with the first really good "Oh shit." When you say "Oh," breath is inevitably drawn in. And when you say "shit"—breath comes out explosively. It may sound a little crude, but it works every time. The patient is breathing again!

Under normal circumstances, the first stage of Griefwork accomplishes the essential task of ensuring that the patient is breathing. It is therefore emergency first aid, but as a long-term strategy there are obvious shortcomings. Usually this initial stage transitions into the next stage, however it can become stuck, and we are all aware of tragic individuals whose life is consumed in endless rounds of shock and anger. Such people are led to a life of imprisoned terror simply because they were never provided the space/time to allow shock and anger to do its job. Fortunately, most of us move on to the next stage, *Denial*.

Denial

The second stage, *Denial*, can be infuriating to bystanders for it seems that those in the throes of grief simply refuse to face reality, and engage in a constant iteration of words and actions which avoid the true situation. They behave *as if* the traumatic insult had never occurred. Workers who have lost their livelihood with a plant closing continue to show up for jobs they will never hold again. In conversation they will talk constantly about the past and show a steadfast refusal to acknowledge the present and move on to some future. And it happens over and over and over again.

It is very tempting to see all such talk as a total waste of time, for surely the spilt milk will never find its way back into the bottle. Of course this is true, but it also misses the essential contribution Denial makes to the healing process. Denial may be likened to a bandage on a fresh wound, or perhaps anesthesia for severe physical trauma. The simple fact of the matter is that the ending, whatever it was (broken marriage, closed plant, toppled government, failed state) is excruciatingly painful. So painful, that without the protection of the clean bandage or the anesthesia—breath would be sucked away, returning the individuals to the prior state of Shock and Anger. Denial provides the space and the time in which to catch your breath.

Long term, Denial is by no means a successful strategy for life, although once again we all know people who live their lives in denial. The sad truth of the matter is that life just seems to stop with the moment of ending. Everything occurring before that instant is reviewed endlessly with a full measure of "if onlys" and "could have beens." The fact that absolutely nothing can change that reality is totally ignored.

But for most of us, this stage of Griefwork eventually passes, given the time and space to make the passage. This is a process that cannot be hurried or bypassed, and each person will have a different rate of progress, but when the course is run, a new stage will be entered. I call this *Memories*.

Memories

When it first begins, *Memories* seems almost indistinguishable from its predecessor. Once again, there is the endless telling of tales, all of which are related to the past. In a repetitive, cyclical fashion the tale is told, beginning with the moment of ending and spreading backward in time and outward in space, eventually including all those who were significantly impacted by the event. For example, in moments of national trauma such as the assassination of John Kennedy, or the destruction of the Twin Towers in New York, every affected individual will remember exactly where he or she was at the fateful moment and what he or she did and felt in the succeeding times. The stories are told and told again in endless profusion and redundancy. But to what purpose?

The central difference between Denial and Memories is a radical change in mood occasioned by the increasing understanding and acceptance that the unthinkable has, in fact, occurred. Whereas Denial shields people from the full pain of the instant, Memories brings them right into the midst of it all. And the seemingly endless cycle of storytelling has a deep and positive purpose. As the story is told, increasingly larger aspects of life are re-contexted by the changed reality. You might have thought that your business would last forever—but that is no longer true, and many hopes and aspirations, once hinged upon that presumption, are now negated, or radically altered. Life has changed, and the extent of that change is now appreciated.

The telling of the tale serves another essential function. As the past passes beneath the storyteller's lens the significant moments and personalities pop into focus. It is a time of assessment and deepening understanding. Destructive behaviors are seen to be such, and true heros and heroines are honored for their contributions. Memories constitute that moment of radical reflection in which the past is acknowledged in preparation for the future. However, before that future may be fully engaged, two additional stages must be negotiated which encompass perhaps the most profound moments in the human experience. I call these stages *Despair* and *Open Space.*

Despair

If there is anything in the human experience, certainly my experience, that hurts more than Despair, I don't have a clue what that might be. When all the Memories have passed, and the tales have been told, there is nothing left but the cold reality of ending. Future plans that had been predicated on the now ended job, marriage, business—all are forfeit. Hopes that looked forward to a time together with a departed spouse, funds from a now bankrupt business to educate the children, or security from a failed state—all have vanished. In their place there is nothing. This is the condition of Despair (literally, to be without hope).

Even worse, Despair is unavoidable. You can't go backward, though lord knows we try. You can't go over it or under it. Despair sits as an immovable black blob shutting out the light and casting sinister shadows on every aspect of living. The pain—sharp and shrill, or silently numbing—is all consuming.

And yet this pain, for all of the agony, is also the source of our renewal. For most of us there comes a point where the intensity is so extreme that we have no choice but to move in the only direction available—straight ahead into the Despair and through it. I have no idea what the precise mechanisms are, or how they work, but when we take the plunge into the belly of the beast, it turns out that there is light on the other side. It also turns out that our pain was largely self-inflicted, caused by our understandable, but futile, effort to hang on to that which has now gone. In the moment that we let go, the pain ceases and we find ourselves in an exhausted but tranquil state.

I have often thought that the Griefwork process was analogous to the process of birth. As a male, I have never had the experience personally, but I am told on good authority by those who have, that birth comes in stages, each being more painful than its predecessor. The final stage is definitely the worst. But it is also the best, for that is the moment of birthing. One of the driving forces in the birthing process is that toward the end of pregnancy, the womb literally becomes toxic. In simplistic terms, the metabolic by-products of mother and child overwhelm the plumbing system, thereby presenting both participants with an interesting choice: Be born or die.

Not to make light of all of this, but seen from the point of view of the baby, the prospects of birth can hardly be appealing. A warm, sheltered environment with constant service in terms of nutrients and waste removal is about to be traded for the totally unknown. And intervening between present state and the future condition is a perilous journey through a dark tunnel, propelled with all the elegance of toothpaste forced from a tube. Nobody in a right mind would choose such a fate—unless there were no other choice.

I understand Despair to be the final moment of a birthing process, not of a newborn baby, but rather of a new life, or way of living. It is truly convulsive, and the choices are so stark as to constitute no choice at all. We could stay with the intense pain, at least theoretically, but most of us will choose pushing through the pain to the release and relief on the other side. We have finally let go. We are ready to move on.

Open Space[20]

The immediate experience on the yonder side of Despair is that of exhausted tranquility. With a final letting go of things as they were, an extended moment of silence unfolds. Speaking personally, I have found such a moment to possess a marvelous quality of timelessness which initially inspires feelings of relief, transitioning to a sense of expectancy. There is an open space, a clearing in life, with nothing present and everything potential.

It is not unlike that magical experience of being in a forest when the first snowflakes of winter fall. If you listen carefully you can almost hear the flakes caressing the leaves on the forest floor, and there is a bitter/sweet sensation which comes with the realization that everything is over, and simultaneously gathering strength

---

20 My use of the words "open space" in this context may confuse, and if you have been keeping track I have used "open space" to refer to three different things: Open Space Technology, the open space of our lives, and (here) a critical part of the Griefwork cycle. This usage is quite intentional as I think they are all closely related. And as a matter of history, the first usage was the present one. When OST came along I called it "Open Space" because many of the same things occurred in that simple method of meeting as took place in the Griefwork cycle.

for the renewal of springtime. It is an open space, the instant of ending and new beginning, the pause between breathing in and breathing out.

I have always found a strong desire to simply sit in this moment, savoring the timelessness of it all. There is no sense of urgency, nothing to do, nowhere to go. The needs and strictures of the now ended job, relationship, or way of life—have all disappeared.

It also becomes clear that this time out of time is a moment of choosing. One could choose to remain in a state of blissful suspended animation, and some people will take this option. Alternatively, one could choose to move on, seeking to realize some of the infinite possibilities. With nothing on the agenda, all paths are open. No guarantees of course, and doubtless some (even all) of these pathways will turn into dead ends. But there is a choice.

Making this choice usually comes in response to a question offered in words, or some event. The question is a simple one with profound implications: "What are you going to do with the rest of your life?" This question may come directly from a friend, or simply appear in the passage of some event, such as the presence of a child, or the rising of the sun, providing mute testimony that life will go on. But what direction?

Indication that a choice to move is imminent will appear in three little words, *I wonder if* . . . I wonder if I can find a new job, new partner, new homeland, new way of life? And when wonder and imagination coincide, space is opened for *Vision*.

Vision

The emerging Vision may be tame or farsighted. If the Vision is simply that we return to normal, effort will be made to quickly restore old relationships and old patterns, or find similar ones. There is a certain obvious comfort in this approach, but also a sacrifice of possible growth and exploration. When the ground is clear, and the space is open, it is probably worthwhile to at least consider some expanded possibilities. Finding something like the old job has the virtue of putting food on the table with a minimal expenditure of time and effort. However, one might ask whether it will really provide the opportunity to realize the unfulfilled person within.

When the choice is made and the Vision forms, it rarely comes in neat packages with clear-cut statements and bullet points. In my own experience it hardly seemed like a choice at all, but rather more of a compulsion, made all the more mysterious by the lack of precision. Compared to some idealized "life plan," this Vision is a mess, more feeling than content, all decked out in the rainbow colors of the mind. But it has one major thing going for it. It is powerful, a source of motivation with the capacity to take one from an old way of living to a brand new one. No guarantees of course. But on a good day, the emergent Vision has all the flash and dazzle needed to attract attention, combined with the internal logic and substance necessary for life on the ground. However, the news is out, and it is definitely good—life is renewed and it is on to the future.

The Griefwork Cycle Considered

Griefwork is an integral part of the process of self-organization in human systems and it works pretty much all by itself. Described in the more formal language of science, Griefwork enables us to pass through chaos, on to higher levels of complexity, more fully responsive to the changing conditions in our environment. The net effect is improved (higher) performance. But if Griefwork works all by itself, why are we still so often in a mess? There would seem to be a spanner in the works, or for American readers, a monkey wrench in the machinery.

Chapter VIII

A Spanner in the Works

I f High Performance is the natural state of a well-functioning, self-organizing system, and the toxic, and sometimes lethal, by-products of self-organization are effectively processed by Griefwork, what is the problem? By all rights it would seem that we need only to allow the fundamental power of self-organization, well assisted by Griefwork, to do the job, and the Holy Grail of High Performance should be well within our grasp. Not occasionally, not as some odd anomaly—but everyday, 24×7. Somewhere, it would seem, there is a spanner in the works.

The clue to the mystery lies in the word "allow," as in "we need only to *allow* the fundamental power of self-organization . . . to do its job." The problem is that for many of us self-organization simply does not apply to the wonderful world of human systems. And even in those situations where we may see the fine hand of self-organization at work (as in the Informal System), we consider the outcomes to be odd anomalies at best, or definite aberrations to be corrected or eliminated. After all, things are happening which were not part of The Plan and definitely beyond the span of control. In a word, it is all about *control*—its presence, absence, loss, and true status.

One of the things we have learned, sometimes very painfully, in the 20-year experiment with Open Space Technology is that the need for control, and every attempt to exercise control, are very problematic. In fact it turns out that there is precisely one way to ensure that an OST will not work, or certainly not work very effectively, and that is for someone (the facilitator or participant) to take "charge" of the affair. Usually the situation arises when it appears that people are thinking thoughts that the officialdom has decreed to be unthinkable, contemplating actions that are definite no-nos, surfacing long simmering conflicts in a noisy and argumentative fashion, or just having fun. Everybody knows, of course, that work can only be accomplished with deadly seriousness. No matter what the initiating circumstance, somebody comes to the conclusion that order must be restored, that it is time to take charge. When such a moment arrives, there is a notable bump in the road which, on occasion, has the effect of derailing the entire affair. But supposedly this was all done for a good cause. After all, if things continued out of control, the results predictably would be disaster. Perhaps.

It is worthwhile noting that I have never seen a situation in which the level of confusion (from conflict, fun, or other sources) exceeded the capacity of the participants to effectively deal with it, and most importantly learn from it. Even in massively conflicted environments, such as the Middle East, this observation holds true. This is not to say that the ongoing discussions were anything but loud and confrontational. To the casual observer it might seem that bloodshed was a definite possibility. Yet never has that possibility materialized, nor was it necessary to intervene in any fashion. In every case, the people found the way to deal with their situation in an effective, productive, and respectful manner.

The Spanner in the Works: The Need for Control

It might be assumed that *control* is the root of all evil. The problem, however, is not control *per se*, but rather an understanding of control which seemingly permeates the majority of our organizations and institutions. When control is presumed to be the property of the one, or the few, through which the many are guided (or forced) into the proper pathways leading to efficiency, effectiveness, and High Performance—I think we are in real trouble. The adverse effects of this situation are compounded when this view of control is institutionalized as the Formal Leadership, with The Leader reigning at the top of the heap. At that point Leadership is equated with control, and control lies centrally in the hands of The Leader. The problem is threefold. In the first place, that sort of control never happens. Secondly, it doesn't work. Finally, the mere attempt to make it work can do substantial damage.

It Never Happens

Control of the sort that some executives aspire to, and many people assume such executives possess, simply never happens. The moment somebody says, "I have total control," you know that they are either suffering from a debilitating delusion, or have indulged in a controlled substance. It just never happens. The reasons are quite simple and straightforward. Absolute control requires a complete knowledge of all possibilities, along with an hermetically sealed system in which nothing changes without executive permission. No human being on earth, and not even a group of very smart human beings (experts), can possess such knowledge, because the level of complexity and diversity, even within a rather simple system, is so overwhelming. And of course the system is never closed, and the adjacent environment is always impinging— with or without executive permission.

It Doesn't Work

For obvious reasons, something that does not exist has little chance of working, but that does not prevent many people trying. And the mere attempt to impose control has an adverse effect on system function. This is not a question of morals or ethics, and control in and of itself is not a bad thing. Problems arise, however, when the control is *external* and *arbitrary*. External, in the sense that it is imposed from outside of the ongoing life of the system, as for example when The Leader attempts the daunting task of "re-organizing" the system. And arbitrary, in the sense that the nature and form of the controls are determined by executive dictate, and not by the internal, emergent process of the system.

Occasionally, external and arbitrary control may appear to work, but in such situations I suggest there is a happenstantial cor-relation between the new organization and what the system was going to do in any event—all by itself. More frequently the new design has little observable effect, perhaps some different names for old functions, but as the old-timers are wont to observe—Same old, same old, and this too shall pass.

It is true that moments arise in the lives of organizations when revolutions, of one sort or another, break out. At such times options appear limited, and a senior executive might justifiably conclude that there is no alternative but to use whatever authority and apparent control to quell the uprising. But this power play really is a desperation play. Jack Chase, one of the best senior executives I have ever encountered, was the Chief Medical Director of the Veterans Administration, a governmental organization of 250,000 employees. Over the several years that I knew and worked with him, I never saw or heard of him nakedly using the very consider-able authority he possessed. One day I asked him about this, and he admitted that there had been times when he felt compelled to use the power play. However, he said, "I always consider such times to be a failure in leadership—my leadership."

Jack Chase clearly understood that serious problems emerge when the effort to gain control is done with vigor and tenacity, not only in desperate moments, but worse yet as an everyday *modus operandi*. In those cases, war breaks out as The Leader seeks to wres-tle the beast to the ground, get his arms around the critter, and impose his will on the recalcitrant organization. Real Control!

As with all wars, there will be winners and losers. Sometimes everybody is the loser. Should the loser be The Leader, he will doubtless retire, lick his wounds, and consider what it was he did wrong—unless he is relieved of his duties. It may never occur to him that the mission had been an impossible one from the start.

Then again, the loser may be the organization as a whole. Even though it may appear that order and efficiency have been restored (chaos, confusion, and conflict eliminated), that appearance is only superficial. As the strictures of external, arbitrary control are imposed, space is closed, and life within that institution can make a life sentence in a maximum security prison seem like easy time. You may feel I have grossly overstated the situation, but my 40 years of working in, and with, organizations of all sorts, in virtually every corner of the globe have brought me into corporate and government environments that make a prison camp seem almost like paradise. To be sure there is no concertina wire stretched between guard towers, and few people actually get shot, but the levels of anxiety, fear, disillusionment, wasted dreams, and desiccated lives is appalling.

Doubtless if you were to question The Leader, you would find that he was doing his very best to apply the most advanced thinking regarding system design, employee motivation, and management technique. And if you asked for the objective the answer would likely come: superior performance—High Performance. Yet it appears, at least to me, that the greater the effort, the worse things get. In the name of quality and performance, controls are laid on, layer after layer—with controllers to control the controlled, and so on down the food chain. If the goal is truly a High Performing System, it would appear that going the way we are going, we are not likely to arrive at our destination.

Peter Vaill, writing in the short paper cited at the beginning of this book, seemingly has similar concerns. He asks—

> To what extent are we managing our organizations in such a way as to prevent the emergence of High Performance? We espouse a philosophy of high performance. Our management literature is full of it. But do we manage and lead in such a way as to achieve High Performance?[21]

You will not be surprised to learn that my answer to Peter's painful question is—No! But I think it is not only a matter of the

---

21 Peter Vaill, *op. cit.*

management and leadership styles, but more fundamentally the understanding of "organization" which underlies those styles. Stated rather bluntly, *Understanding a self-organizing system to be something we organized is a misunderstanding of major proportions.* If it is true that there is no such thing as a non–self-organizing system, then our efforts at organizing (read imposition of structures and controls) are at best gratuitous, and at worst represent a real spanner in the works.

It Can Do Substantial Damage

The extent of the damage done, or potential unfulfilled, may be seen in a comparison between the sorts of behaviors and experiences found in the average Open Space gathering, where self-organization is the order of the day—and what might be called a "typical command and control" organization. I admit this is a bit of a caricature, but if the truth comes through, so be it.

HPS/OS Style	"X" Company
High Learning	Rote Learning
High Play	No Play/All Work
Appropriate Structure/Control	Arbitrary Structure/Control
Genuine Community	Prison Camp
Authentic Leadership	Dictator

High Learning, you will remember, refers to those paradigm busting moments where insight breaks through. This may be contrasted with endless training programs which require the rote retention of facts, figures, and procedures. Doubtless such efforts have their place, but if they constitute the sum total of learning, it is small wonder that innovation is often a stranger.

High Play is the antidote to dogmatic thinking and therefore an essential companion to High Learning. It is also fun. In "X" Company, play is strictly prohibited, for after all there is work to be done, and it is always very serious. Even worse, Play, almost by definition, is out of control—which is what makes it fun. Can you imagine anything worse than playing a game where the results were always known in advance? Boring!

Appropriate Structure and Controls points to the fact that robust mechanisms for effective work emerge naturally from the people themselves, all in tune with the task undertaken and the environment. Arbitrary Command and Control comes from above and squashes the life out of the organization. Under the best of circumstances the external and arbitrary imposition of structure and control is a simple annoyance, and the "old timers" will quickly devise work-arounds. Under the worst of circumstances such efforts are positively lethal.

Genuine Community sprouts naturally in an environment where people do what they care about, and care about what they do. Prison Camp may stretch the truth a bit, but not too far if you listen to the repeated refrain about being anywhere but at work. As they say, "Thank God it is Friday!"

Authentic Leadership emerges from the passion and responsibility of those who care (Nexus of Caring), creating focus and direction for the emerging organization, and a nutrient space in which that organization may grow. Diversity of opinion is honored as a rich resource, and new Nexi of Caring are welcomed as the natural and organic seeds of growth in the living organization. The Dictator, on the other hand seeks to control it all, deeply suspicious of diversity, and threatened by emerging (authentic) Leadership.

The "spanner in the works" then is our search for control, but the problem is not control in itself, but rather our *search*, and the need to impose *our* version of control on a self-organizing system. Even with the best of intentions, the control we attempt to impose is *external* in that it comes from outside the system, as opposed to emerging naturally from the system itself. And because it is our version of control, it will inevitably be *arbitrary*, in the sense that it will accord with the nature and processes of the system only by chance. The reason is simple, the system in all of its aspects constitutes a level of complexity totally beyond our capacity for understanding. Under the best of circumstances our attempts at control will make little difference, and the system will continue on its own way. Under the worst of circumstances, our attempts at control will be so vigorous as to disrupt normal function, and effectively bring the system to its knees.

Extrication

So how do we get out of the mess we are in? The way forward does not lie in the elimination of control, for controls are essential to all human systems. Rather it is in the release of our *need* for control and the attempts to gratify that need. It is all about *letting go* —*but not giving up!*

There are, in fact, multiple things that we can do to enhance the function of our systems, and to enable the achievement of true High Performance. But none of them have anything to do with designing the system, or controlling it. The organization design, and the inherent controls, are all emergent and they will happen pretty much by themselves. We can, however, create conditions under which this is most likely to occur in positive and productive ways. Further, we can perform essential maintenance and support functions which we might call the Care and Feeding of Self-Organizing Systems. Lastly, we can experience fulfillment and success (High Performance) for ourselves and our organizations by learning to leverage the power of self-organization. Like surfers, who must understand that they are never in charge of the wave, and yet can ride that wave with competence and grace, so may we find the High Performance we seek. In short, we may become skilled and effective Wave Riders.

PART II

The Wave Rider's Guide to the Future

I t would be a gross error to view what follows as the definitive version of *The Wave Rider's Guide*. That book remains to be written, but I believe you will find more than sufficient material with which to get started, all presented in a practical stepwise manner. Beginning with the fundamental mind-shift necessary to see the world as a Wave Rider must see it, on through Eight Essential Steps for the fulfillment of the role, I have attempted to deal with the basic questions—What does it mean to be a Wave Rider? What do Wave Riders do? Subsequent editions of The Guide may describe ten steps or only seven, but this journey—as all journeys —begins with a single step.

Chapter IX

Becoming a Wave Rider: The Care and Feeding of Self-Organizing Systems

The task from this point onward is to apply what we have learned about self-organizing systems and the ways in which they may be consciously initiated and sustained. The goal is increased levels of performance for our organizations and our personal lives. The short take on all this is: When superior performance is desired—Open Space. This is not about "Doing an Open Space Event," although there are certainly occasions when that might be the appropriate approach. Rather it is about the continuous opening of space in a variety of situations and circumstances. With sufficient space, the natural power of self-organization will do its work, not just in the circumscribed conditions of "an event," but 24×7—365 days of the year.

Although there are a number of things that may be done in support of this objective, none of them include choosing self-organization as a *modus operandi*. That choice was made billions of years ago. From that moment forward all systems are self-organizing, including our own. Truthfully, we all recognize this fact of life, if only intuitively, witness our participation in the Informal Communication system. We all do it, but guardedly, and usually with a twinge of guilt. It seems that we are not playing by the established rules. But who among us has not heard a piece of "good gossip" which led to some useful action on our part? We may, however, avoid the guilt and the surreptitious missions to find Lucy. The alternative is a conscious choice to align ourselves with the fundamental power of self-organization, and to leverage its potency in support of our goals.

Starting Point: A Mind-Shift

It all begins with an open mind which permits the possibility of a genuine mind-shift. The mind-shift is the familiar figure/ground reversal. In this case the figure is the Formal (organized) System, and the ground the Informal (self-organizing) System. For most of us, for as long as we can remember, the Formal System, depicted in all of the organization charts and manuals of procedures, has been the dominant image. The Informal (self-organizing) System has remained in the shadowy background. Indeed in most cases, that background has been so faint as to be un-noticeable, and if noticed then disparaged. We all knew the true nature of the system, and how it got that way. We did it. A reversal is required.

What was perceived to be marginal and inconsequential needs to be moved in our thinking to the place of dominance. In a word, it is self-organization all the way down. Not a little bit, not just on the fringes—but from top to bottom, beginning to end.

I am reminded of the old story of the king who came to his wise man with the question: "Upon what does my kingdom rest?" And the wise man answered, "It rests upon the back of a fierce lion, your majesty." And upon what does the lion stand? "Oh, your majesty—the lion stands on the broad back of an elephant." "I see," said the king, "and upon what does the elephant stand?" "A turtle, your majesty." "And the turtle. . .?" "Oh, your majesty, it is turtles all the way down." Switching metaphors—It is self-organization all the way down.

Figure/ground reversals are difficult for many people, and this particular one may verge on impossible for some. Despite our best efforts, the old dominant figure pops back to dominance. If this is your experience, I believe you may at least start the process by taking the reversal in the manner of a "thought experiment."

As with any thought experiment, the power and utility becomes apparent (or not) only when tested. So in this case, just suppose, for the sake of the argument, that it really is self-organizing all the way down, and then see if there are substantial elements of your life experience that make more sense from this point of view. For example, do previously anomalous occurrences now appear almost predictable, if not in detail, then at least in form and function? If you suddenly discover the mystery surrounding such things as the emergence of high performance in odd places and times tending to resolve so as to become natural and not so strange—then it may well be that the new viewpoint has some validity.

For me the most obvious example is a typical day in Open Space (Technology) where it seems almost routine that unlikely people do impossible things, all within a breathtakingly short period of time. Viewed from the perspective of Formal System dominance, such an experience is questionable to say the least, and probably illegal, immoral, and maybe fattening. On the other hand, with the benefit of the suggested mind-shift, what takes place in the ordinary OST becomes understandable, and even predictable. If OST is not part of your experience base, then perhaps the gastronomical delights of New York City and the curious fact the 8.5 million people are generally well fed, and some exceptionally so—with absolutely nobody in charge—may appear somewhat less than a miracle.

If the delights and effectiveness of the New York feeding system does not work for you, you might recall those experiences of utter frustration in the face of the Formal System. Salvation appeared only when you and your colleagues devised clever "work-arounds," those time honored devices created when failure is about to be snatched from the jaws of success by the voracious Formal System. You may then be well on the way to a full appreciation of the Informal System, and not terribly far from a time when the proposed figure/ground reversal holds more often than not. Welcome to the Underground—the world of self-organizing systems!

No matter how you get there, making the shift is essential. One can scarcely take care of a self-organizing system until it is recognized. But more than recognized—given primacy of place. It is self-organization which provides the context, the setting for everything we do. Even in those circumstances where we work very hard organizing some project—the moment it leaves our hands it becomes just one more piece of that self-organizing world. This is not a matter of choice. It is not about *becoming* a self-organizing system. Self-organizing is what we are, and have always been.

Three Caveats to Help You on Your Way

As we make our way in our self-organizing world, three simple caveats will be helpful. What they may lack in elegance they more than make up with practical utility. The Three Caveats are: (1) Never work harder than you have to. (2) Don't fix it if it ain't broke. (3) Never, ever, even think you are in charge.

(1) *Never work harder than you have to.* We are workaholics, and when we run out of things to fix and problems to solve, the incipient feelings of guilt drive us to make up new problems and search for more broken things. As a rule for living, this approach leaves something to be desired, but in a self-organizing world the results can be even more difficult. The title that some of us carry, Manager, suggests that we should be spending our time organizing and controlling things. Unfortunately, self-organiz-ing organizations organize themselves, and are always out of our control. The net effect is that we spend a lot of time and energy doing things that need not be done. Furthermore, organizing a self-organizing system is not only an oxymoron, it will very likely throw a spanner in the works. This sad ineffi-ciency squanders energy resources that will definitely be required to effectively sustain and maximize the impact of the self-organizing systems of which we are a part. While it is true that much of what we used to consider our essential tasks is no longer necessary, it is also true that in order to realize our full potential much will be required in terms of focus, pres-ence, and skill.

(2) *Don't fix it if it ain't broke.* This little gem comes from the deep wisdom of the Great State of Maine, and its folksy exterior veils its profound utility. In this present context we are reminded to spend some useful time appreciating the actual operation of the human systems we encounter before ever thinking about

improvement. In most cases we will find that the system has its own inner wisdom which has evolved over time to enable its "fitness" with the environment.

A marvelous example of the system's wisdom at work is the informal communication system, the home of Lucy and her friends. Usually referred to in disparaging ways (gossip, radio office), and often repressed by the powers that be, the system is in fact a marvel of communication. It is time to make friends with Lucy!

Some years ago a client came to me with what he termed a "communication problem." It seemed that the messages were not getting through. Upon arrival at his place of business, I asked this simple question: "How long did it take for the last thoroughly bad piece of news to move from one end of the corporation to the other?" The answers ranged from "a day" (from those who had not been in the office at the time) to "instantaneous"—the common response from those in The Lucy Loop. My conclusion, which I shared with the client—the system is working perfectly, but there may be some problem with the content.

I grant that my statement could appear flippant, but I think there is a real point. Were we able to effectively utilize the informal communications system—useful information could pass with something approaching the speed of light. It may also be noted that despite our best efforts at suppression, the informal system will continue to function. More importantly, when it comes to "source credibility," watercooler gossip trumps the official memo every time—because "Everybody knows . . . ." So rather than fight the (informal) system we might better learn to flow with it. Perhaps things don't happen the way we might expect, or as all the books tell us they should—but if it works, it works. And for goodness sake, don't fix it if it ain't broke.

(3) *Never, ever, even think you are in charge.* The last caveat is the most important. Given our education and life experience, being in charge/control has assumed the position of a major goal. The typical employee evaluation form, for example, asks three primary questions: How many people do you control? How well do you do that? And how long have you done it? If the answers are: a) Lots b) Totally and c) For a long time—you clearly deserve the corner office and the title of CEO. And of course, to be out of control is to be out of a job. Enter the reality of self-organization, in which control as we have understood it is impossible, and worse—the mere effort to establish such control is counterproductive at best, and often leads to disaster. For most of us, there is a sharp learning curve ahead, and keeping this caveat in mind will protect us from a world of trouble.

For High Performance—Open Space!

If we have learned anything during the past 22 years working with Open Space Technology, it is simply this: When performance falters, or increased levels are required—Open Space. Typically this has meant using the tried and true approach of inviting all those who care about the issue at hand to sit in a circle, create a bulletin board, open a marketplace, and go to work. We have also learned that the "magic" is not the approach itself, but rather the fundamental power of self-organization. While it true that Open Space

Technology has the demonstrated capacity to release the power of self-organization, it is clearly not the only way to go for the obvious reason that self-organization is not the special gift of OST. Long before OST was created, self-organization was alive, well, and doing its job. Thus as we move our attention from the more limited confines of a single event toward the larger world of everyday organizations, it seems reasonable to remove the middle man (OST) and simply apply the lessons learned.

Eight Essential Steps for the Care and Feeding of Self-Organizing Systems

Taking our lead from the ongoing experience with Open Space Technology, the process of self-organization can be enabled and sustained by paying careful attention to eight critical steps. Perhaps there are more steps or fewer, depending on how one counts, but these eight essentials have proved their worth.

1. Do Your Homework Before You Start.
2. Extend an Invitation.
3. Come to the Circle.
4. Welcome Passion, Responsibility, and Authentic Leadership.
5. Remember the Four Principles.
6. Observe the Law of Two Feet.
7. Keep Grief Working.
8. Formalize the System.

Chapter X

Step 1 *Do Your Homework Before You Start*

Befor beginning any journey it is useful to consider where you want to go, why you want to go there, and what might happen along the way. Initiating (or renewing) an organiza- tion, particularly a high performing organization, is a journey of a different sort, but with all the same prerequisites.

Under the old rules, we might call this creating a Business Plan, but plans have the unfortunate connotation of being something that will be implemented, and in extreme cases there is the implica- tion that somehow The Plan creates the future. Given the nature of self-organizing systems, the notion that the future will be created by our plan is a little absurd. So if we have to call the product of our efforts anything, I would suggest Business Intention.

Where do you want to go? This first question might also be phrased, *What do you really care about?* The object of your quest may be large or small (a whole new business or some relatively minor improvement), but until there is some clarity about its nature, the likelihood of reaching the goal is rather small. But clarity is only part of the equation—it must be complemented with *caring*. If the goal is simply a good idea that somebody else finds attractive, it will remain at the level of "good idea," until it has heart and meaning for you.

When clarity and caring come together, you will be ready to start. However, if either or both are missing, this is a trip you should not take.

Why do you want to go there? Or in slightly different terms, if you reached your goal, what would have happened? What would have been achieved? What difference does it make? This is the opportunity to be more specific about your intentions and expectations. And of course, should it turn out that nothing will happen that makes a difference, this would be good and sufficient reason to stop right there.

What might happen along the way? Presuming that your evaluation has come out positively thus far—you are clear and committed about your destination and believe it will make a difference—the next step is obviously to consider what you will be needing for the journey. At this point we come to the practicalities of the situation: funding, physical resources, and most important—people. Who should be invited to join you in this adventure?

Very obviously our list of requirements could be a lengthy one, and the needed time to prepare it a long one indeed. If we are not careful, however, we may find ourselves in that dreadful condition known as Paralysis by Analysis, and while we are preparing our lists and charts, the wonderful opportunity that we have clearly seen and committed to simply disappears. To add insult to injury, it may seem that we have forgotten a most important element—how are we going to get organized? According to the old rules, absolutely nothing of utility can happen until the organizational design is in place. And we haven't even thought about that critical design!

At this point we arrive at a very interesting moment. In the world of self-organizing systems (the only world we have, I believe), organization will emerge (or not), and no amount of effort on our part to "organize things" will have any useful effect. Under the best of circumstances, our efforts will be a waste of time when the emergent organization overcomes our design. In the worst case scenario, our attempts to impose our design on the emerging system will have the disastrous effect of throwing a spanner in the works. But the question remains. Can we really afford to trust the process?

The blunt answer to this question is simple. We don't have any choice. Even worse, there are no guarantees of success. For those afflicted with high levels of risk avoidance, this is not a pleasant moment. However, several considerations may make this situation more palatable. Primary among these is that, at this stage of the process, the level of committed resources (our exposure) is limited to nonexistent. Certainly our egos may be on the line, after all this is our project. But the pocketbook is secure. The second consideration is that the process has basic go/no go choice points as it moves along. And with each choice point a rising level of resource commitment will be required. However if the choice is no go, that is pretty much the end of the story.

Presuming that we do not choose to stop before we truly start, the next step is to begin assembling the elements from which our emerging system may grow. This has little to do with funds and equipment. It is all about people. And the question is, who should be invited to join us in the adventure? We need a guest list—but a guest list that includes more than the usual suspects, our familiar peers and colleagues, acknowledged experts, and potential funders. Under ideal circumstances we should invite everybody who *might* care to join us.

Chapter XI

Step 2 *Extend an Invitation*

ffective self–organization in human systems starts with vol–
untary self–selection in response to a genuine invitation.
This contrasts dramatically with the common practice in
which the manager in charge identifies the needed individuals and
assigns them to a project. While this makes sense given the tradi–
tional understanding of the nature of organizations, it is the direct
antithesis of self–organization.

A genuine invitation is one that can be refused. And to what–
ever extent the invitation is actually a veiled command, space is
closed and the likelihood of fully functional self–organization
diminished. One might think of the old joke in which the manager
says, "I need four volunteers—You, You, You, and You!" That is not
an invitation!

A real invitation carries certain risks. After all, people might
choose not to come. But it also carries a genuine benefit, for it
assures that those who do come actually care to come. Caring, or
personal commitment, carries with it an essential ingredient for
superior performance in any project, which is the passion of those
involved.

A skeptic might remark that if everybody did only what they
cared to do, very little would get done. But a brief reflection on the
true conditions operative in the last "assigned project" you were

involved with might yield a rather different conclusion. Let's suppose that Manager X had just initiated Project Y by assigning five people to the task. However, once the project begins, ask yourself who actually did all the work? It is quite likely that of the five assigned, only two individuals bore the burden of the task. The other three found innumerable reasons why they just could not take part. Perhaps the reasons were all good and true, but the attendant feelings were not of a similar flavor. Each time the threesome heard about the project, or worse yet had occasion to meet the two hard workers, pangs of guilt made themselves known. And on the other side of the fence, the two hard workers felt resentful. Even if the project was accomplished on time and within budget, the presence of resentment and guilt does not enhance the quality of the workplace. And over time, resentment and guilt will poison the environment yielding what some call a toxic workplace.

Perhaps this toxicity is just another cost of doing business, but if it could be avoided, ongoing levels of performance can only improve. One way of eliminating the guilt and resentment would simply be to invite participation rather then command it. It is more than probable that the two individuals who eventually did the work would have accepted the invitation in the first place, leaving the other three to perform useful tasks that they cared for. Task done, and toxicity avoided.

Then again, things can work out differently. Take the worst case scenario—that the invitation was extended, but nobody came. Even this is not necessarily the end of the world. It could be, for example, that the proposed project was actually a bad idea. Or that the people were really busy doing other good things, and that given a little discussion, ways may be found to work in the project so that it could be accomplished effectively. The critical point is that the collective wisdom of the full system (in this case the 5 people + the manager) can be invoked to solve the problem. This can never be the case if external and arbitrary control is employed from the start. System power fails when self-organization slows or ceases, and a spanner is found to be clogging the works. It all begins with invitation.

Of course, we still have what might be called "the nasty things"—those unpleasant tasks of organizational life that *nobody* really wants to deal with. How would an all-volunteer force deal with that stuff?

My experience has been that there are three possibilities, any one of which will deal with the situation. First is the fact that "nasty" is a personal perception, and what I may find to be super nasty, other people rather enjoy. Case in point would be accounting. I certainly enjoy money and definitely like to keep track of it, but when it comes to the business of accounting, I would infinitely prefer a trip to the dentist. Fortunately there are any number of people for whom accounting is a real pleasure, and on a larger scale—with 6.5 billion people in the world, there is a high likelihood that somebody somewhere will care for the job. This fact argues for extensive communication with the environment (other people), and a high degree of diversity in the organization.

Another possibility is that the perceived "nasty" can be eliminated if people are given the freedom to think about it. On the other hand, if the "nasty" falls within the category of Standard Procedure, which must be followed because it has always been followed—the choices are limited. Owen Corning Fiberglass had a real "nasty." Fiberglass is, as the name suggests, thin fibers of glass, which under the best of circumstances are itchy, scratchy, and painful for human beings. And more than an annoyance, the stuff is actually hazardous to your health. Standard Procedure dictated that large bats of freshly manufactured fiberglass would be handled by human beings under conditions of high temperatures and humidity. That was the way it was always done, until a group of workers and the supervisor had a different thought. Why not wrap the stuff in heavy paper? Of course that would cost money and it wouldn't really improve the insulating qualities of the fiberglass— but a definite "nasty" would be eliminated. This novel idea was put into action and surprisingly, costs came down. The cost increase for the paper wrapping was more than offset by a massive increase in productivity. People could do a lot more when they weren't distracted by the itchy-scratchies.

The final possibility is that the people who care, as only true volunteers can care, will take on a nasty for the good of the organization. Case in point is the manufacture of synthetic detergents. I am told by those who know about such things (I don't) that the chemical composition of a synthetic detergent is dangerously close to the formula for high explosives. Extreme care in the manufacture of these detergents is therefore essential lest there be a most embarrassing, to say nothing of destructive event. The situation is compounded by the fact that in the most critical areas, the manufacturing process is hot and can be dusty, making working conditions less than ideal. Increased compensation (hazardous duty pay) is one approach that has been tried, but there is a down side.

People who are doing it only for the money may not have their heart in the job.

A radically different approach worked wonders in one plant. Everybody was invited to volunteer, and of course only those with the required skills could do the job—and for those whose skill level was too low, special training was offered. Taking a turn at the critical place (referred to by all as "the pointy end of the stick") became a mark of honor, which served to increase the number of volunteers. At the end of the day, people who really cared effectively took care of the nasty.

Who Should Be Invited?

Who should be invited? The simple answer is: Anybody who *might* care to come. I admit that sounds pretty sloppy when compared to the more traditional approach of inviting only a small select group. After all you could get a whole bunch of malcontents and incompetents. However, you are also more likely to get a broad diversity of viewpoints and a large amount of passion for whatever the task at hand.

Diversity will make the solutions more robust, and the ambient passion will drive the whole affair, even if it is a little bit chaotic, confusing, and conflicted. As for the malcontents and incompetents, there may be a few, but judging from our experience in OST, such people rarely have sufficient energy and focus for followthrough. They may think they will show up—but somehow never quite get around to it. Even if some of these "less desirables" do make an appearance, the ambient energy of the group as a whole may well inspire unexpected levels of performance. On the other hand, that same ambient energy may just overwhelm the "undesirables" to the point that they find it necessary to seek alternative space. Either way the problem solves itself without doing damage to the integrity of the process.

And don't forget the stranger! It is quite understandable that those who are making up the invitation list should restrict their choices to known quantities—people of their acquaintance whose skills and work habits are already demonstrated. Understandable, but very limiting, especially if the new venture is to break out into unknown territory. People who think and do what they have always thought and done, carry few surprises. And surprises are often viewed as anathema for the management of a well-executed plan. At least that is the conventional wisdom, but the conventional wisdom is often confined to conventional results. Thinking outside the box, and more importantly getting there, will require the services of someone who lives there—outside the box.

Consider the example of Rockport Shoes, a relatively small American corporation known for making outstanding casual shoes. Rockport Shoes had done very well for itself, but it knew it could do better and different.

With such thoughts in mind, the whole corporation gathered to "Build a Better Rockport." When things got started, a major concern was "New Products," and some 70 people met to address that issue. Ideas were flying in all directions and while this was happening a hired security guard, (not a Rockport employee) passed by on his rounds. Unexpectedly, he took a chair and inched his way into the group, stopping only when he sat face to face with the Vice President for Marketing. Shaking his finger at the surprised

executive he said, "Why doesn't Rockport Shoes sell shoes to security guards? I'll tell you why. They don't look right!"

Rockport makes beautiful, comfortable, casual shoes. Security
guards, who probably spend more time on their feet than most
other people, require formal footgear. It could well have been that
the VP for Marketing would take offense. After all, he was the VP
and this was "just" a security guard, and not even a Rockport
employee—a stranger to be sure. But to his credit, the VP understood in a flash that this stranger had just identified a very large
market that Rockport had totally overlooked. And the fix was easy
and obvious. It you have a good shoe, making it formal is a matter
of cosmetics. The chase was on!

A small group detached itself from the larger body and raced
to the Shoe Lab where they made prototype models for the product line. Simultaneously, the VP for Manufacturing consulted with
some of his people searching for available manufacturing space.
And the VP for Marketing was circled with his people developing a
marketing plan. Of course the security guard was a central consultant. But the best part was the CFO, who was busy with the backs
of all available envelopes figuring the ROI. Bottom line? $24 million
in the first year, and it happened all because of a stranger.

Chapter XII

Step 3 *Come to the Circle*

T he circle is critically important for the initiation and support of self-organization. And so when individuals are invited to participate, the geometry of meeting must be a circle. This may be a circle of the mind, what I might call the image of organization, or a real time/space circle of chairs, but a circle nonetheless.

The images of our organizations, which we hold in our minds, radically affect behaviors and organizational function. Were I to ask for the picture of your organization it is likely that you would describe the standard organizational chart—with the CEO at the top and all attendant personalities and functions arrayed like roots beneath. Granted that this picture is probably out of date, it nevertheless strongly influences the way we think about, and actually perform, our jobs all of which shows up in the language we use. For example, if we get a new position we say, "I went up the ladder" or "took a lateral transfer," or (God forbid) "went to the basement." When a decision is required, we might say, "I have to go up for a decision," and by the same token, when implementation is the order of the day, the words come out—"take it *down* to the folks." With this picture in our minds, life at work becomes an exhausting scramble up and down the organization chart.

Of more import to our present discussion is the fact that the space described is a very restricted and channeled sort of space.

There are pathways, but only predetermined pathways, precisely the wrong sort of space for self-organization. This is why the Informal System devotes much of its energy getting outside of the pathways, "back-channel" so to speak. A well functioning self-organizing system requires the maximum amount of free, open space in which to create its own pathways.

It is interesting to note that participation in the informal organization is often referred to as "being in the circle." Participation in the formal system is usually referred to as "being in the hierarchy." Political insiders have always known that regardless of your position in the hierarchy (or lack of same), being in the "inner circle" is a prize plum. In a word, circles beat hierarchies every time.

If we change the image in our minds from the standard organizational chart to a circle, we will experience a radically different working environment. All of our associates are now positioned around us at eye level. The space which separates us is free from obstructions. When it comes to engaging each other for productive activity, the pathway is straightforward and the energy required (at least psychic energy) is reduced to a minimum. We all know that the shortest distance between two points is a straight line. Simply by changing the image, we eliminate a tedious task: following the complex zig-zags of the organization chart.

Mind games for sure, but mind games with a point. The circle is the geometry of communication, and free, open, and rapid communication is the lifeblood of a self-organizing system. At stake is the adaptive capacity of the system which enables it to effectively engage in the ongoing search for fitness within itself, and externally with the environment. When communication is restricted, needed information fails to materialize, and the system is locked in a holding pattern. In a circle, exposure to incoming stimuli from the environment is maximized because the surface area available for contact is large, and infinitely better than the limited points of contact available in the tiered organization, which may be reduced to a single point labeled Corporate Communications. And internally, the potential for communication is also maximized.

To see the importance of geometry for communication we need only think of what happens to people when placed in different geometries. When sitting in rows schoolroom style, with the teacher at the front, the power situation is obvious. The teacher is in charge, and all the students subservient. The only possible behavior is a passive/aggressive response to one way communication. Obviously genuine discussion is limited, for who can feel inspired when talking to the back of somebody's head? Not incidentally, the schoolroom configuration is simply the old organization chart on its back with The Leader at the front. The effect on interaction and communication is the same: limiting.

With a square, or rectangular table, the mode of communication shifts to that of negotiation which often becomes adversarial. We find ourselves talking about "your side" and "our side." However placed in a circle, people will communicate, all at once, all the time. Perhaps only with a glance or a cocked eyebrow, but under some circumstances there is more than sufficient meaning in the simple act.

And it is not all mental models. Physical circles of people are very rich and productive, as became apparent to the good people of the Bank of Montreal when they found their circle somehow violated. The bank had utilized Open Space Technology in a variety of circumstances over a period of years and, as often occurs in such cases, the customs of Open Space spread quietly to the broader aspects of their work life. Specifically, they started to rid themselves of tables in their regular meetings—just a circle of chairs.

One day the regular conference room was unavailable, and so they borrowed a conference room from a corporate neighbor. This conference room came equipped with an aircraft-carrier-sized board table. Upon arrival everybody naturally sat down, but now separated by the monstrous piece of wood. The meeting itself was just a normal affair with no particular hot issues on the agenda— and yet by the time it was over everybody was in a completely foul mood. Minor points were endlessly and heatedly debated. Tempers rose, productivity disappeared, and everybody departed noting that this had been the worst meeting they had in years. Several days later, when tempers had cooled, it came as a common, blinding flash of the obvious. It was the table!

Chapter XIII

Step 4 *Welcome Passion, Responsibility, and Authentic Leadership*

Whole person is welcome. So often it seems that we only want the "nice" part of people to participate in our projects. And it can go downhill from there, to be limited only to the socially acceptable "business face," suitably garroted by the appropriate tie (for the male of the species). The real issue is diversity, and when people in an organization look, act, and think as if they came from a common cookie cutter, diversity is limited to a crippling degree.

Of course, there was a day when the conventional wisdom decreed that efficient and effective operations depended on everybody thinking the same, acting the same, and all singing from the same song sheet. Variance was to be minimized, if not eliminated. At that point, diversity becomes an enormous problem to be fixed. However, as we have come to understand the nature and mechanisms of self-organizing systems, we have learned that without high levels of diversity, in all the ways that diversity may be understood, the entire operation may come to a gooey halt, mired in its sameness.

The required diversity is not only a matter of skin color, education, economics, or culture, but also the peculiar and particular differences in each individual, manifest in what they truly care about, what excites their passion. Passion is the source of our creative energy, and in its absence, such essential things as breakthrough innovation and true inspired performance take a holiday.

That said, it is also true that passion requires some degree of focus, lest its power be dissipated in wasteful ways. External controls tend in that direction, but more often than not they are too clumsy and hamhanded. They lack the sensitivity and fine tuning necessary to bring powerful passion to a laser point of effectiveness. The true balance can only be achieved by the exercise of internal controls, through the assumption of personal responsibility.

The appearance of personal responsibility is rarely the product of demands for accountability, even less from the imposition of assigned responsibility. Ultimately personal responsibility arises when people care to assume it—and *care* is the operative word. At this point the presence of passion becomes critical, and of equal importance the object of that passion—which is what people truly care about. Here the circle becomes complete. When whole people are invited to come with their passion(s)—what they care about— they will assume personal responsibility. Genuine responsibility cannot be given, forced, or commanded. It will only appear by way of invitation.

A short story may make the point. A number of years ago I was the Executive Director of the Adams Morgan Community Council in Washington, DC, where every Christmas the community (which really meant the local merchants) would erect, and lavishly decorate, a Christmas tree. The resplendent tree was truly a gem and attracted attention from all sorts of people, some of whom did not seem to have the spirit of Christmas in their minds.

Each year the level of vandalism increased, and no matter how much the local teachers begged their students to be responsible, and the police patrolled to enforce that responsibility, it just got worse. Finally the benefactors thought to distribute their bounty in some other way. There were to be no more Christmas trees. Just as we were to run out of time, I met with the merchants and asked for one more chance, but I suggested that we do things in a different way. If they would erect the tree, I would take care of the decorations.

As it happened I had been working with a gang of neighborhood kids who, I strongly suspected, were largely responsible for the vandalism, and if not them, then their acquaintances. At the next meeting of the gang, which usually took place in my storefront office, I made a proposal that we should decorate the tree. I was greeted with quizzical looks and stony silence, but several days later boxes of all sorts of shiny stuff began to appear in my office. By the weekend we had more material than Santa's workshop. I didn't ask too many questions about where it had all come from, but on that Saturday, the whole gang showed up and we set to work. I can't say that the product was finely wrought, but I do know that the ornaments produced were made with love, care, and no small amount of dark humor. By Sunday we had enough to do the tree, and by nightfall it was fully decorated.

The level of vandalism was reduced to zero, and as a matter of fact if somebody even thought about doing something to that tree, that thought was quickly banished from the offending mind. It was all about taking personal responsibility for something you care for. And it worked.

Authentic Leadership

Passion and responsibility have another gift to give—Authentic Leadership, which provides the critical focus and direction for the emergent organization. But please note—this has nothing to do with the appearance of The Leader. In fact the net result will be a plethora of leaders, each creating the nodal points of organization, the strange attractors, the Nexi of Caring.

The conventional wisdom has understood that a multiplicity of leaders creates confusion which can only be resolved by the singular vision of The Leader. All other leaders are to be subordinated, or eliminated. We have any number of colloquial phrases to make this point: Too many cooks spoil the broth. There is only one captain of the ship. My way or the highway. Is it any wonder that many organizations find leadership in short supply, and that when new leaders are sought, they all seem to have disappeared? The truth of the matter is leadership in general, and emergent leaders in particular, have been suppressed from the start. There is one right way, enunciated by The Leader who maintains the course by strict command and control. To be sure multiple efforts are mounted to "train and create leaders," but I think this is a clear case of working much too hard. We have only to invite passion and responsibility—and leadership, Authentic Leadership, will appear in abundance.

But how do you avoid the "herding cats syndrome"—where multiple leaders go off in myriad directions? As every cat lover knows, Mr. Cat will come when he cares to come, and herding cats is not only an oxymoron, it is impossibile.

Obviously, this is no idle concern for you and your new venture. However, Mr. Cat can show you the way. Cats come when they care to come, and your task is to create the conditions that are sufficiently attractive. With cats, the provision of dinner will generally suffice, and a gentle scratch behind the ears can help. Human beings tend to be a little more complicated, but the approach is similar.

When you extend your invitation (Step 2), you effectively put your own passion and responsibility out in public view, you create a Nexus of Caring. To the extent that others find this invitation attractive, they will choose to join you in the adventure, bringing their own passion and responsibility. Whether or not they choose to stay and contribute substantively to the emerging enterprise depends ultimately on their continued caring.

People obviously care for many different things, and some-where along the line, some of us concluded that the major thing was money. If we pay people enough they will care to come, stay, and align themselves with the business at hand. Unfortunately, study after study has shown that, while important, levels of com-pensation come in pretty low on the scale of motivating (care inducing) factors. Well ahead of the size of the paycheck, such things as respect, challenge, sense of meaning, opportunity for growth, appreciation for their contributions—rise to head the list. These factors appear initially in the form of a genuine invitation to bring one's whole self—all the passion and responsibility. These factors will continue in evidence so long as the invitation is con-stantly renewed. Invitation, in short, is not a once done thing, and Michael Herman and Chris Corrigan, two young colleagues, made a significant contribution when they coined the phrase, "The Inviting Organization." Continuing invitation is a major key to organizational longevity.

The invitation to bring passion and responsibility is an invitation to Authentic Leadership—lots of it. Authentic Leadership creates the nodal points of caring, the strange attractors around which a living organization grows and evolves. This is not a static, cast-in-concrete affair (the old organization chart with The Leader at the pinnacle), but rather a constantly flowing dynamic field. Some of these people will hold their place for a long time, but not because they have some inherent right. Other people will come and go as they find new things to care for. Well done, the ambient flow will have the power and coherence to sustain wholeness, health, and harmony—the essential ingredients of a High Performing System.

Chapter XIV

Step 5 *Remember the Four Principles*

The Four Principles, announced at the start of every OST, go as follows: (1) Whoever comes are the right people. (2) Whatever happens is the only thing that could have. (3) Whenever it starts is the right time. (4) When it's over it's over.

The principles in OST do not tell people what they should do, but simply acknowledge what will happen in any event. In a word, they are descriptive and not prescriptive. One might ask why state the obvious? The answer is that many people who first come to OST, find the situation to be strange, counterintuitive, and even wrong. We announce the principles to alert them to what will be happening, and hopefully make them feel more comfortable. And of course, what is "happening" is not so much OST, but rather self-organization. It is for this reason that I suggest that remembering the Four Principles when consciously working in the larger world of self-organizing systems will be helpful.

Whoever Comes Are the Right People

It is typical at the beginning of any project, large or small, that much time and effort is devoted to selecting the "right" people. No small amount of anxiety is produced when some or all of those "right" people fail to make an appearance. The situation in the world of self-organization is a lot different and in many ways much easier. It turns out that whoever comes are the right people.

This assertion may strike you as preposterous, even outrageous. What on earth could make (or ensure) that they are the right people? Answer: The simple fact that they *cared* to come. As previously noted, complexity science has described a wonderful thing called a Strange Attractor, which provides the "catch point" around which the odd chaotic elements coalesce, initiating the process of self-organization. Human systems possess an analogue, the Nexus of Caring. People care about many different things, but a group that cares about the *same* thing tends to come together (organize). When those who care coalesce, the odds are very strong that useful work will begin, which makes those people by definition the *right* people for the job.

There is always a natural tendency to count heads, and should it turn out that only a few people cared to come, when we might have expected hundreds, this is not a disaster. The critical issue is not how many bodies, but rather how much they care. History is replete with examples of small groups of caring folks who have moved mountains. And for sure they will outperform a much larger group that could care less. In this regard, we might remember the dedicated, underground crew which gave us Post-its.

Of course, there is always the possibility that nobody will care to come. If the nascent self-organization is your new business start-up, this state of affairs could be rather a shock. However, as painful as it might be, there is some useful information here. If nobody cares, the likelihood of a successful outcome is minuscule. Knowing this before major resources are committed may be a blow to the ego, but it is a positive advantage to the pocketbook.

Whatever Happens Is the Only Thing That Could Have

Obviously the grammar of this principle is somewhat tortured, but the intent is very straightforward. Do not worry about all the things that might have happened, could have happened, even should have happened—focus on this present moment because that is all there is right now. This is not to suggest that reflections on the past and hopes for the future have no place or purpose, but the simple truth of the matter is that the past is over and the future hasn't happened yet. All we have is *now*. And perhaps more to the point, if our minds are filled with memories of the past, or dreams for the future, we are very likely to miss, or fail to fully appreciate, what is taking place right in front of our eyes.

A clear focus on the present moment is critical for our lives as self-organizing systems, or as the people at the Santa Fe Institute would say, Complex Adaptive Systems. And the key word is "adaptive." To achieve the highest levels of performance (find the most effective degree of fitness with ourselves and our environment) it is essential to be in constant, conscious contact with the infinitely complex and changing world. The complexity theorists have taught us that even within a nanosecond slice of time the degree of complex interaction is absolutely mind-boggling. Of course, much of this passes well below our capacity to notice, which may appear fortunate for our peace of mind, however, it is also a liability. Even the smallest changes can represent the foretaste of emerging advantage or disaster. In the mythology of the chaos folks—this is the fabled butterfly flapping its wings.

It turns out that full, conscious awareness of the present moment is no easy thing. Viewed as a rational project in which we might identify, track, analyze, and respond to the myriad elements of our existence, it is simply overwhelming. That said, conscious attention will raise the odds for a successful outcome, and every little bit helps.

Whenever It Starts Is the Right Time

This principle seems designed to drive all conscientious managers to distraction. After all, keeping things on schedule, with precise start and stop times, would be considered by many to be a—if not *the*—central task of a good manager. However, it is a fact of life that nothing has ever started on time or ended on time. Close, even very close, but never "on time." This fact of life may be seen most obviously, and perhaps painfully, in all conferences. The posted schedule may look absolutely glorious on paper, carefully laid out in 5 minute increments—but the reality is starkly different, and the common lament is soon to be heard. The conference is running late!

The difference between the posted schedule and life on the ground is precisely the difference between the formal system and the informal/self-organizing system. And the informal system trumps the formal system every time, as all meeting participants know full well. Fact of life: Things start when they start.

There are also deeper implications here. When we attempt to force the informal (self-organizing) system into compliance with the dictates of the formal system, we pay a price in terms of innovation, creativity, and levels of performance. Innovation and creativity happen when they are ready, and never according to the clock. Speaking personally, I find that the harder I try to be creative the

less likely I am to achieve my goal. Inspiration breaks through on
its own timetable.

Regarding levels of performance, we might recall Peter Vaill's
Behavioral Characteristics of High Performing Systems. According to
Vaill, High Performing Systems have a light regard for the clock
and even more pointedly, "External controls on the activity of the
HPS are seen by members as at best irrelevant and at worst as positive impediments to performance." This does not mean that HPS's
are anarchists, but rather that the sense of time, structure, and controls are emergent and internally generated. And when external
controls are enforced, the level of system performance will likely
decline, if only because added layers of management are required
for enforcement (controllers to control the controllers and so *ad
infinitum*). System performance further degrades because productive
members (those who actually do the work) now have to invent
work-arounds to do what they were going to do anyhow. Worst
case scenario is that they will actually spend all of their energy
defending against the formal demands—at which point system
performance degenerates to zero. All of these negative possibilities
may be substantially avoided by simply remembering that *Whenever
it starts is the right time.*

At precisely this moment you may well be thinking that what I
am proposing may sound interesting—but for sure it would be a
hell of a way to run an airline, or any other complex, mission-criti-
cal system. In the airline business, being on time is important, and
keeping on time assumes something of the status of the First
Commandment. This is all true, but we need to ask: Whose time are
we talking about?

There is, of course, the Official Time (Schedule), but that turns out to be only a starting point which must be adjusted in relation to a number of other "times," such as Passenger Time, Maintenance Time, and of course, Nature's Time.

Passengers are supposed to be at the gate when it is time—and if they aren't, they are left. Well, most of the time. But if it happens that a passenger's bag has been loaded on the plane, but the bag's owner has been seriously incapacitated, forgetful, or lost, the plane will sit until the passenger arrives—or all the bags must be unloaded in the name of security.

Maintenance Time runs on a different clock which starts at the moment mechanical malfunction is discovered. Maybe the problem will be fixed on time, but it will always be fixed in its own time. And no matter the official schedule, everybody will agree that it is better to remain on the ground a little longer than to meet the ground unexpectedly.

Nature's Time obviously trumps all other times. Given a piece of nasty weather Passenger Time, Official Time, and Maintenance Time all take second place. And following the Established Rules and Procedures when nature contravenes can lead to inconvenient results as JetBlue (a new, small American airline) discovered to its pain and embarrassment.

JetBlue boasted of on time departures, but Nature had conjured up a massive storm along the East Coast of the USA. Nevertheless JetBlue planes left their gates on time—only to sit, and sit, and sit on the taxiways, in some cases for 5–6 hours. When they finally came back to the gates, all the gates were full, the passengers were furious, and the total system broke down in complete disarray.

Other (older and wiser) airlines simply canceled flights, and when the storm abated, they were ready to fly. JetBlue had blown it and remained in confusion for the better part of a week. Even with airlines it is true: Whenever it starts is the right time.

When It's Over It's Over

This simple statement recognizes a fact of life. Everything under the sun has a beginning, middle, and an end. And when the end comes it is best to acknowledge the fact and move on. This is not to suggest that at the first sign of trouble one simply walks away. As we have noted previously chaos, confusion, and conflict are all essential and integral to the process of life as a self-organizing system. And each of these brings with it the necessity for hard work and struggle through which enhanced levels of performance may be achieved. It is all about the Search for Fitness—but there comes a time when things just do not fit any more. The life form has run out of steam—it is over.

At such a moment, the Griefwork process begins. As it runs its course healing takes place and new life is a possibility. However, the emergence of that possibility will be delayed if we continue to hold on to what was. In essence this aborts the process and leaves us stuck with Denial, Memories, even Despair. There is no chance of avoiding any of these stages, unpleasant as they may be. But there is a possibility of allowing the process to run its natural course, and even accelerating the rate of passage. And all of that begins with the simple recognition that—When it's over it's over.

Avoiding this principle adds tragedy to tragedy. When some organization reaches the point of ending, the strategies and activities

undertaken in support of its continuance are multiple and exhausting. I am reminded of the final days of Eastern Airlines. When that
venerable operation reached the end of the road it seemed that the
level of strife between labor and management reached new highs.
Each competed with the other for a slice of the pie, without seeming
to recognize that the pie had already been eaten. Management
looked for more secure "golden parachutes" and Labor was negoti-
ating for lifetime contracts. In point of fact, it was all over, and the
parties involved might better have spent their time considering
where to go next.

Chapter XV

Step 6 *Observe the Law of Two Feet*

T he Law of Two Feet specifies that if at any time you are neither learning nor contributing, you should use your two
feet and move to a more productive place. In OST this may
first appear as a curious, possibly quaint, affectation, but its application in the larger world of "real" businesses and organizations
seems something of a stretch. The immediate assumption is that if
everyone were to follow their own personal predilections the
resultant chaos would be disaster.

Seen from the point of view of those who consider the formal,
organized system to be dominant and desirable, such a judgment is
doubtless correct. On the other hand, when the mind shifts, and
the ground reverses with the figure, so that self–organization is
understood to be the fundamental reality, chaos becomes an essential precondition of emergent order. No chaos—no order, no life, no
organization. More to the point, all attempts to limit, or eliminate
chaos are not only doomed to failure, but are actually counterproductive. Chaos, we are learning, is the rich seed bed of emergent
order. Strange new world.

Remember that the Law of Two Feet is descriptive, although it
is certainly phrased in a most *prescriptive* fashion. In truth, we all
follow the Law of Two Feet regardless of constraint or intention.
When learning and contribution cease, interest dissipates, and our

capacity for caring finds a new locus. That locus may be out the window with the birds, into the middle of next week for that exciting conference we anticipate attending, or backward in time to the beach last summer. The fact is—we are no longer present, nor do we care to be present.

In the world of self-organizing systems, the Law of Two Feet is a simple statement of fact—but remembering to observe that law will have a more than salutary effect on the optimal function of human systems. The reason is a simple one. When we become prisoner to the strictures of the formal system (custom, regulation, procedures, ways of thinking about things), all of which may have been very good ideas once upon a time, we are effectively taken out of the ongoing search for fitness. As individuals we will lose the opportunity to build new skills and new competencies. And the organization of which we are a part will lose an effective agent (us) in the ongoing pursuit of high performance. In a word, it is a lose/lose situation.

Under optimal circumstances, when the Law of Two feet is fully observed, we become part of a milling crowd, randomly searching for a better way to be (fit). From the point of view of the conventional wisdom, being a part of the milling crowd appears as a perfect prescription for ineffectiveness, the very antithesis of high performance. And yet, as we may learn from our brother the ant— a random search is the epitome of efficiency provided there are a lot of searchers and an effective means of rapid communication.[22]

---

22 See Kevin Kelly, *Out of Control* (Addison Wesley, 1994, p. 306 ff).

When morning comes, and the colony is in need of sustenance, the ants stream out across the local real estate. What begins as an orderly column quickly dissolves into a random search pattern as each individual ant is guided in new and different directions by the local topography and its own particular abilities and limitations. There is no formal grid search, and each ant is on its own, doing its own thing. Collectively they cover a lot of territory very effectively, and sooner or later they will discover their objective: food. You might say they were following the Law of Six Feet.

Food may come in the form of some unfortunate worm, or perhaps our picnic lunch, but once the discovery has been made, the randomness of the crowd quickly transforms into the ordered progression of worker ants bringing home the bacon. And the key to the transformation is effective and rapid communication, which in the case of the ants seems to be chemically based, but it surely works.

To say that the ant behavior is random is by no means the same as saying it is aimless. Each ant knows perfectly well what it is looking for: dinner. In our own situation, as we wander amongst the milling crowd, the randomness of our search is focused by what we *care* about. And conscious attention to the Law of Two Feet ensures that we keep that focus. Sometimes, to be sure, the Law operates in an apparently negative fashion by allowing us to leave what we *don't* care about, but this process of elimination may be the only way when life becomes confusing and overburdened.

In sum, the Law of Two Feet keeps our attention on what we really care about, what has genuine heart and meaning for us. When we lose sight of what we care about, we lose our compass,

and of course, if we care about too many things, the effect is essentially the same. At such a time, being clear about what we *don't* care
for can be clarifying.

The image of large groups of people randomly seeking what
they care for throughout, not only physical space, but also what I
might call "possibility space" (much of what we seek will never be
found at a physical time/space coordinate)—is awesome indeed.
Given an infinite number of random possibilities, how on earth
could anything approaching an orderly, purposeful, life—individually or collectively—ever emerge? Stated more practically, how could
we ever get organized to conduct the business at hand when the
mode of operation appears as massive, hedonistic anarchy?

The secret is our old friend, *Nexus of Caring*. As people search for
what has heart and meaning, some number of these searchers will
discover that they are looking for the same thing. This commonality of caring draws them together much as the Strange Attractors of
Chaos Theory draw together the oddments of the physical world,
and with a similar result—emergent order.

Traditionally, creating order (organizing things) seems to take
forever. In the world of self-organizing systems the experience is
radically different. In the early days of research on the subject, Ilya
Prigogine noted that the transition from the "old order" to the new
one was virtually instantaneous. One minute the teapot exhibited
random swirls and bubbles, and in the next instant the new
ordered pattern of a rolling boil put in its appearance. Order out of
chaos—in the moment.

The 20-year experiment with Open Space Technology suggests
that something similar takes place in the realm of human systems.

You will recall the 2108 German psychiatrists who created and scheduled some 234 workgroups. The numbers may be impressive, but the time it took to do the actual organization may appear unbelievable. Following a brief introduction by the facilitator, the group created their agenda, defined working groups in terms of participants and of time and place of meeting in less than one hour. This may not be quite instantaneous, but compared to the standard lead time most conferences of that size and complexity require, it is pretty close.

The process of self-organization moves from chaos to order with sometimes blinding speed, provided the system is not locked in a predetermined pattern. Which is only another way of saying that the system will quickly adapt so long as the Law of Two Feet is observed. However, should that system become bound by arbitrary, outdated customs, rules, or procedures then it will quickly ossify. Solution? Keep the feet moving!

Chapter XVI

Step 7 Keep Grief Working

I t is a fact. The process of self-organization proceeds with what, in other situations, is called *collateral damage*. As things naturally move along, the forces of chaos, confusion, and conflict do their essential work, and some inescapable level of destruction occurs. Chaos rattles the old order, giving new opportunities a chance to emerge. Confusion muddles made-up minds, putting dead certainty at risk, so that fresh ideas may make their appearance. And conflict knocks off some rough edges as it sharpens our ideas and hones our levels of performance. All good, all useful, and all attendant with some degree of pain—which at times can be excruciatingly severe.

Fortunately for us there is the Griefwork process. For as long as human beings have been human, this process has been doing its job. When trauma occurs, the process begins quite automatically, and if it runs to term, which is the usual case, the pain of ending is transformed into the joy of a new beginning. Through Shock/ Anger, Denial, Memories, Despair, Open Space—we eventually are swept to Vision. Truthfully we might have wished for some alterna- tive, or even to be able to escape the entire thing, but so far no alternative has surfaced, and escape does not seem possible. We did not design it, certainly don't run it, and in the majority of cases,

Griefwork takes care of the business all by itself. But it is absolutely essential that it keeps doing its job, and we can help.

Knowledge of the Griefwork process is very helpful. This is more than an academic exercise because understanding the stages and impact of Griefwork will majorly assist our own navigation, and our ability to help others along the journey. A rather trivial example will make the point.

Twenty odd years ago when I was writing my first book, I reached the point where I was to describe the Griefwork process as it related to organizations. I began early in the morning and wrote all day—my fingers just flying over the computer keys. I was convinced that I was doing something of large importance and became so wrapped up in the effort that I forgot to save my work as I went along. My computer was one of the very early "lugables" running on CPM—and totally bereft of such modern conveniences as "automatic save." As I hit the final period on the final page of a truly inspired performance—the power went off. Nothing but a blank screen.

When the power came back, the computer booted up, and I was still gazing at a blank screen—but now with some very strong feelings! My first words were predictable, and you know what they were, followed almost immediately by a frantic search of the files. I just knew my "disappeared" chapter had to be there somewhere. Denial was doing its work. And then I found myself, head in hands, desperately trying to remember what I had said. Memories had arrived.

At that point I started to laugh, because it really was funny. There I was writing a chapter about the stages of Griefwork—and found myself going through precisely that process. However, my knowledge of the stages proved very helpful. It was clear that I had to let it all go before I could move on. Sitting there trying to remember what I had said could only be an exercise in futility. Even if I could have recaptured most of the words, I would have lost the essential passion and flow. But my knowledge of the process saved me from all that. Instead I simply shut off the computer, went for a long walk, followed by a drink and dinner. And the next morning I started all over again. I really believe my second effort was better.

As painful as my little experience may have been, I learned a great deal. First I discovered how even the smaller traumas of life initiate the Griefwork process—although to a writer, losing a whole chapter doesn't feel very small. My second learning was probably more important. By recognizing the stages as they passed by I was able to save myself considerably. When I reached the point of letting go—I carefully and intentionally did just that. The alternative could have been much more painful, perhaps spending the night searching for all those beautiful lost words.

Griefwork is something that each one of us must do for ourselves. And even when a whole organization is grieving for some major loss, it is a journey that nobody can take for another. But we can and must help.

Previously I compared the Griefwork and birthing process. This comparison is helpful, I think, enabling us to understand better not only the process itself, but also the assistance we might render to those who are on that particular journey. The first element of understanding is that the birthing process will proceed with, or without, our assistance. But the process can be facilitated, which is the role of the midwife. The midwife does not conceive the baby, nor will she give birth—but she can be very helpful along the way.

The midwife brings two vital elements to the situation. First is an understanding of the process, and the second is her presence. An understanding of the process assists the mother in maintaining some sense of place and purpose.

The process of birth, as also Griefwork, is unpleasant at best and a real pain at worst. And pain in large quantities is disorienting. There appears to be no before or after—just an unending, excruciating Now. Changing any of this is not an option, but to the extent that the mother can be reminded that there are stages along the way toward birth, albeit each stage is worse than the preceding one—there is real possibility of keeping her eye on the goal, a new baby.

The physical presence of the midwife is probably the most important thing. This is not about *doing* something, although technical assistance can be helpful, it is really about simply being there as a warm, caring companion on a difficult journey. Holding hands definitely helps because physical contact can cut through the pain when words fail.

The juxtaposition of "Griefwork" and "midwife" may seem rather odd, if only because grief is the product of ending and death while the midwife is concerned with birth and new life. And yet I think it is appropriate, for the Griefwork process in its totality also leads to renewal and new life. In short, it is the built-in mechanism which brings us through the vicissitudes of life occasioned by chaos, confusion, and conflict as they contribute to the ongoing process of self-organization.

Like the birth process, we did not invent it, cannot change it, but we can assist our colleagues as they move through the process of grieving.

Specifically, in the time of Shock and Anger we can make certain that there is sufficient time and space for both Shock and Anger to come out full force. Granted this can be a little disruptive to the tranquility of the neighborhood, but if the process is constrained, worse yet aborted, the likelihood of a positive outcome falls close to zero.

A number of years ago I had as a client Owens Corning Fiberglass during a very painful moment in that corporation's history. This was the time of the corporate raider, and one of these carnivores had set upon Owens Corning with a vengeance. The hostile raid was successfully resisted, but at a great cost. To satisfy the stockholders, lawyers, and bankers, the management found it necessary to sell off, or close down, just about one-half of the corporation. In a six week period, Owens Corning went from a $4 billion per annum giant to something half that size. Not everybody lost their jobs, as many people went with the businesses that were sold. But many people did find themselves among the ranks of the unemployed, and those that remained were more than a little worried that their time was next. It was indeed a very painful moment of ending on a rather large scale.

I was requested to see if there was something to be done to help the survivors, and so I found myself in a large room filled with silent and exceedingly stressed people. I have no idea what they thought was going to happen, but I am positive nobody suspected what actually took place. Upon entering the room, I stood quietly for a moment, and then with a soft voice asked what might have seemed an impertinent question under the circumstances. "How do you feel?" I said—and was greeted with total silence. I repeated my question perhaps two or three times, and always received the same silent response. After yet another iteration, I heard a very quiet, almost strangled, voice from the far corner of the room. It said, "Oh Shit." Putting my hand to my ear, I said—"Let's hear that again." And once more the magic words broke forth, this time with a little more intensity. Again! I said—and pretty soon we had a rousing "Oh Shit Chorus," with full participation from all assembled. When the decibel level rose to a stadium-filling quality, the tone shifted dramatically from an angry chant and turned to laughter. Smiles spread across faces for the first time in days. Even in a particularly dark time, it was funny and the laughter itself was very therapeutic, and for very much the same reason that the Oh Shit Chorus had been previously. You have to breathe in order to laugh.

With the appearance of Denial, there is not much to be done, and certainly we must refrain from the natural attempt to make people face the facts of ending. It is true that the milk has been spilt, that the failed organization/state/relationship has definitely failed. However, the pretense that all is as it was, serves a major purpose, providing a momentary release from the pain. A chance to catch your breath.

When Memories flow, there are a number of things that we can do by way of assistance, not the least of which is to provide a suitable environment in which those who grieve may tell their tales. This could be a rather formal setting, as in the Irish Wake, or something infinitely less formal like a gathering of friends for a cup of coffee. No single approach will work in all situations, but no matter the approach chosen, it must be appropriate to the people involved and their unique history.

Some years ago I worked with a U.S. Army unit which had been designated for dissolution. For many of those who had been intimately involved with the unit's program the experience had been profound, and for some, life changing. They viewed their work with pride and saw its termination as a disaster, not only for themselves, but for the Army as a whole. Needless to say there were others who did not share that assessment, and unfortunately the disbelievers were in the ascendancy. Net result—the unit was soon to be history.

The Army has a practice known as After Action Briefing. Whether the action was combat or something less exciting, the participants will assemble for a Lessons Learned session. For the most part the format is a pretty dry technical review of what happened, didn't happen, or might have happened. But inevitably, as the Lessons Learned are considered, the Story is told. I am not sure that anybody ever thought of this particular activity as being an integral part of the Griefwork process, but consciously or not, it certainly has that effect, particularly if the action in question was violent and costly combat. It was therefore very natural to do an After Action Briefing at the point of the unit's termination.

Accordingly, present and prior members of the unit were invited for a weekend gathering. The Friday evening began with the reading of the formal orders of termination issued by the commanding general, and effective on that date. It was now officially over.

On Saturday morning we sat in a large circle, OST style, to address the theme, "What have we done, and Where are we going?" Topics were identified, groups formed, and for sure the Story was told. The day passed in deep conversation marked by moments of belly shaking laughter as humorous events of the past were recalled—along with moments of silent sadness in honor of people, programs, and events that had passed away. In large part, the discussions focused on the past, things once done and never to be repeated. But the future also broke through as people contemplated their next steps, new careers, new interests.

By evening the mood had shifted considerably. The termination of the unit was generally accepted as an accomplished fact. The heros and events of the past had been acknowledged. The leading edge of the future had put in an appearance. By dinner time, some sort of celebration seemed almost inescapable. Toasts were offered, speeches given, and by the end of the evening the group seemed ready to let go of what had been a deep and meaningful experience and prepared to move on to whatever was coming next.

For many people, perhaps most of the time, once the stage of Memories has been negotiated, they are ready to let go of the prior situation and to get on with life. This seems to have a lot to do with the level of trauma suffered, or looked at in a slightly different way, the degree of attachment. For the Army people only casually connected to the unit, its passing was not a life changing event. On the other hand, there were a few individuals whose life had been profoundly affected by their association with the unit and its work. For these people, the unit's demise was of more than incidental concern, and once the Memories had been shared, they found

themselves in a very cold and forbidding place known as Despair.
It was time for the final letting go of something that had redefined
their lives.

When the loss is a small one, as for example the lost chapter of
my book, the moment of Despair may pass with hardly any notice.
However as the stakes are raised, so also the depth of the Despair
increases. For major trauma—the loss of a loved one, a life work, a
way of life—the Despair may appear as impenetrable darkness, and
the ambient pain simply overwhelming. At such a time it is quite
understandable that we should seek to protect those who suffer.
But to do that is counterproductive. The agony of Despair cannot
be avoided, it can only be passed through—and we can be present
with our brothers and sisters in the moment of passage. Like a
good midwife in the final moments of birth, we may urge the
afflicted onward, and also provide just about the only assistance
possible—a gentle touch.

Once past Despair the space opens into a silent clearing with
nothing present and everything possible. As I have said, this is perhaps the holiest moment of human experience, and when given the
privilege to share such a moment, I find that my own humanity is
deeply confirmed. It is for this reason that not only *can* we be of
assistance in the process, but we *must* do so. The reason is equal
parts self-interest and altruism.

We may also have the opportunity to ask the critical question:
What are you going to do with the rest of your life? Please note, it
is always a question and never a statement. The question provides
the Open Space of possibility into which the person (or organization) may choose to enter. We cannot make that choice for them,
although we might dearly wish to do so.

In our desire to be helpful, and perhaps also deal with our own anxiety in a time of ending, it seems natural to rush in with detailed plans and suggestions. For individuals it will seem reasonable to point out new career possibilities which may fill the void left by the recent termination, or whatever else may have occasioned the onset of Griefwork. If it is a whole organization which has reached the quiet point of ending, the natural tendency would be to offer a new strategic plan—the vision for the future.

As natural as all of these good offers may appear, they are ill advised for a variety of reasons. First, in the initial moments in Open Space, it is quite unlikely that even the most powerful suggestions will be seriously heard. In fact they may be perceived as an intrusion in a very private and profound moment.

And that moment is a significant one. For the first time in possibly a long time there is a genuine respite from the normal business of the day. Suddenly all of the usual demands are put on hold. Meetings to attend, calls to answer, new product to ship out the door, all of that has ceased. Some people will find the silence all but unbearable, but it is rich with possibility. When everything is gone, anything is possible, no longer precluded or constrained by the way things were. No longer does the rush of activity prevent serious contemplation of fundamental questions such as: Where are we going and what would we really like to do?

Presuming this is a business, the cold breath of economic necessity can make staying in the moment appear something of an unwarranted luxury. Truthfully, nobody would have chosen such a situation, but now that it has arrived it is not to be wasted. Plans and strategies devised before their time in response to some deep

sense of anxiety are quite likely to be shallow, stopgap, and ineffective. And for sure they will lack the robust nature that deeper
thought can provide.

For most individuals and organizations, there will come a time
when moving on in a new direction is a natural step. And emphasis should be placed on the word *natural*—for the process is in fact
an organic one. Not unlike the process of birth, it has its own time
and its own pacing, and little if anything can change that without
serious consequences.

Intimations that moving on is imminent typically come with
the appearance of three little words: "I wonder if. . ." I wonder if we
can find a new product, business, way of life, mission? When first
uttered, these words are perhaps more in the nature of idle mus-
ings, pretends, what ifs? But over time, they assume a degree of
clarity and urgency. When that time arrives it can be an invitation
to real dialogue, an opportunity for direct participation. At the least
you can be a sounding board, and perhaps you will be able to
offer concrete suggestions and proposals. But you can never offer a
finished plan, or even less, the suggestion (or veiled threat) that the
plan be adopted. To do so is to strip the newly emerging self-
organization of its integrity and a return to the old approach of
organizing a self-organizing system. Never worked, and it won't
work now.

The appearance of wonder and imagination (I wonder if. . .)
provides the fertile ground for the emergence of Vision. In the early
moments, the content of the Vision is far from clear. Perhaps it
hasn't quite come into focus as yet, or multiple possible visions are
flipping by like a slide show. Once again there may be a natural

tendency toward impatience for those who sit in the spectators' gallery. Pick something! Do something! Get on with the business!

But there is a method in the apparent madness of the evolving Vision. Possibility Space is being explored. To some extent this is a rational, linear process as potential opportunities are considered and discarded. However, when the line is crossed between possible visions and The Vision, the driving force is infinitely more powerful than the logic of rational analysis. The genesis of this driving force may be a little hard to determine. Some will identify "the gut" or simply say that it feels right. But no matter the source it is clear that passion has appeared, and with it the felt sense of responsibility for the new direction.

With the appearance of passion and responsibility a new invitation is also extended and the age old process of self-organization of a new (or renewed) human system has commenced. In essence we have returned to the beginning. Remember—everything starts with invitation.

This invitation may never appear in the standard format: *The pleasure of your company is requested*—but it is an invitation for all of that. When passion and responsibility put in an appearance, a new Nexus of Caring is established which is attractive and inviting, but differentially so. Simply put, some people in the vicinity will find it appealing (they care about the same thing) and others won't (they could care less). The importance of this phenomenon to the emerging organization cannot be overstated. A vision which manifests in the mind and heart of a single person, or even a small group, may be interesting, but it will only become viable as others choose (voluntary self-selection) to join—either as participants or supporters. But it all starts with invitation.

When Vison appears and the invitation is extended, the natural next step is Celebration. The word celebration might suggest a formal occasion with speeches and awards, which may be appropriate in some situations and cultures, but frankly what I have in mind is a little more earthy—a real party. Indeed this is a special party for all those who care, or might care, about the new business or venture.

Taking time for a party at the moment of organizational "lift-off" may appear to be an unwarranted waste of that time, considering the multitude of things to be done. But it will be time well spent. Obviously this party will not celebrate organizational successes, for they have yet to come. But it is the celebration of the conclusion of a process, a cycle of life, which has gone deeply. From the stark moment of ending through Shock, Anger, Denial, Memories, Despair, and on into the opening space of new possibilities—the new, emergent organization has now arrived.

Most organizations celebrate something, but all too often that "something" is almost of trivial concern, and certainly not related to the deep history of those who have journeyed together. Several years ago I received a curious call from a client. The message was that his "Christmas celebration parties were a disaster." And he wanted to know if I could help. I visited his place of work, and in a very short time the culprit was identified. It seemed that some 95% of his employees were Jewish. Wrong celebration for the right people.

Celebrating the wrong thing, or not celebrating at all, represents a serious loss, for celebration is, and should be, an occasion to participate in one's history and contemplate one's future. It is a time for telling the story, honoring the heros, renewing the spirit. For old-timers the time can be sweet, a remembrance of prior accomplishment and an opportunity to share dreams for the future. For the newcomers, such a celebration offers the chance to participate in the history—not just know the facts, but actually *feel* the impact, if only vicariously. It may also be the time in which their dreams may be woven into the unrolling fabric of the organizational life.

Celebration of the Organization's life events is always important, and first among such celebrations is to honor the primal moment when life begins, or is renewed. It is all about history *and* the future. It is very difficult to know where you are if you have no idea where you came from, and little idea of where you are headed. Genuine celebration gets you *There*—to that exquisite instant when past accomplishment and future expectation converge, otherwise known as The Present. For the newly emerging organization, firm grounding in the present moment is essential, for there is much to be done, and no time like the present to get started. Having a good party is a great way to begin.

Facilitating the Griefwork process is a key aspect of the Wave Rider's role. When leading their organizations to higher levels of performance, there are few things that can make a greater contribution. Even in very ordinary, mundane circumstances, there will inevitably be any number of painful endings. As the world might see such things, these endings appear small and even trivial, but for those involved the picture is quite different. A simple closing of a department, denial of a promotion, disapproval of some pet project, is more than sufficient to set the Griefwork process in motion. After all, I lost only the chapter of a book! But as long as the process continues, the people who are intimately involved are, to some significant extent, taken out of the action and can make little or no contribution to the performance levels of the organization. And should the process abort, or simply get stuck, the cost to the total organization can be considerable. The net result is an abundance of what I might call the walking wounded—those survivors of unresolved endings. Instead of contributing positively to the organization's growth and development, they remain locked in Shock and Anger, separated from the present by Denial, or in the worst case scenario, prisoners to unending Despair. Even a very small number of such people constitutes a heavy load for the most robust organization. And the answer is quite simple: Just keep Grief working.

Chapter XVII

Step 8 *Formalize the System*

Y ou may have thought that I had forgotten all about the Formal System. Not true, but the order of consideration is just the reverse from the traditional procedure. Conventionally, we would start with organization design, proceed to implementation, and then engage in an ongoing series of "fixes," otherwise known as re-organizations. In the world of self-organizations all the "heavy lifting" of system design and implementation is taken care of by the system itself. That is why it is called Self-organization. But there is still much work to be done.

In the earlier discussion of the formal system I suggested that it was exceedingly useful in boundary situations—those points where the system comes in contact with the external world. For the customers, there must be a plainly marked Complaint Desk, banks will be happier when they can see a position marked Treasurer. For the newcomers, there must be sufficient connect points to get them started along the path to becoming a good employee, until that happy day when they discover Lucy. For all of this to occur in some efficient manner, good maps and signage are essential, but the maps must reflect the territory and the signs must be clear and well placed. But in no case will the maps create the territory.

The need for the formal system is real, but best met in moderation, which may be achieved by constantly asking the question,

"What is the minimal level of formal structures and procedures necessary to sustain system function?" And less is always best. Unneeded structures and procedure will only get in the way of the ongoing process of self-organization. At best they are an annoyance, and at worst they may slow everything down in a gooey mess of bureaucracy. All this may be accomplished by paying careful attention to *how* the system is organizing and then creating, in a minimalist fashion, formal structure to support and sustain organizational function.

An example may be helpful. A number of years ago, when there was a massive expansion in the State Universities in the United States, it was common practice to design and construct the whole campus, and then allow the students to enter. Design and construction included the work of landscape architects and engineers who created the roads and pathways for the campus, but when the students actually showed up, the result very often was not what one might have anticipated. Although there were paths and roadways in abundance, sometimes even marked with signs, the students typically went any way they wanted to go. In a very short period of time, new paths were cut through landscaped gardens, producing what many considered a terrible mess. However, no matter the number of signs (Keep off the grass!) and fences erected, the student body (a totally self-organizing system) went where it would.

Sanity was eventually restored, and enormous amounts of money saved, thanks to a blinding flash of the obvious. Bring the students in first, let them create their own paths, and then simply pave the beaten paths.

Creation of the formal system begins with a careful observation of the system as it has organized itself, bearing in mind that the system will already have created a number of connect points as it evolves and grows. To the outside world and to the newcomers, these connect points may appear rather strange, or have names which will not be found in the standard corporate vocabulary. But if the functions are being performed, there is no need for redundant layers of organization, although normalizing the nomenclature and changing the look to a more conventional appearance could well be in order.

Case in point was the regional office of a small systems engineering firm known as Veda. The office was located in a most unauspicious setting over a Chinese laundry. For all its limitations, it was clearly a well used workspace, but decorated in a style which might be described as a cross between Jackson Pollock and Andy Warhol. Random splashes of paint dribbled down the walls, interspersed with project management charts and cartoons of Veda employees and favorite clients. By any reasonable standard, the office was a mess, made even more so by the fact that the walls themselves were temporary and had been moved on multiple occasions, witness the nail holes in the floor. The situation, however, was about to change as Veda was moving to a new and glamorous setting. Surprisingly, nobody was very happy about the move.

The unhappiness grew in part from a sentimental attachment to the old place, but there were practical reasons as well. The walls actually depicted the history of the organization and when new employees joined, their orientation to the Veda mission and culture occurred almost by osmosis. As they sat in the rooms, every picture, splash of paint, or set of nail holes in the floor became the occasion for telling the Story—which the old-timers were most happy to do. Leaving behind this source of inspiration and education was not a happy thought.

As it turned out the building was going to be torn down, and the landlord was quite pleased when the Veda people offered to take their walls with them. Once in the grand new office building, the ancient artifacts were respectfully mounted on the walls of a large, freshly painted room with a prominently displayed entry sign: *Corporate Museum and Employee Orientation*. Proper names for a previously existing, self-organized function, and while the new setting lacked something of the old atmosphere, the essential purpose was continued.

Creating the formal system for a large organization is infinitely more complex than this simple example, but I think the process is essentially the same. Let the system show you where and how it chooses to function, and then optimize that function in the simplest and most cost-effective fashion.

When seeking to understand and map the nature of the emergent organization it is well to remember that structure will appear even in the first instants of the organization's life. The word "instantaneous" may not apply, but compared to the amount of time and effort required under the old rules where we did all the organizing, the rate of organization approaches light speed. From the instant the system begins to self-order, structures and process are springing into being. Thus even in the wonderful party celebrating the arrival of vison and the launch of the organization, the ordering process is already well under way.

The shape of this emerging organization may be difficult to perceive, but it will be there nonetheless, appearing in the swirls and patterns of conversations as participants remember their history and consider their future. Some groups will be fascinated with new products, others focus on the financing, while still others find themselves in deep discussion about manufacturing sites and potential employees.

Presuming that the organization lasts longer than the celebratory party (and some won't), focal points of interest (Nexi of Caring) will have been identified and linked through emerging, or existing, networks of relationship. Organization for sure. Thus even in the first moments, the power of self-organization is doing its job, and when it comes to structures and procedures, both are already present. These structures and procedures need to be taken into account as we engage in the formalization (mapmaking) of the enterprise.

A fatal step at this point is what I might call "organization by checklist." In its basic form, this approach starts with the organization design of some similar business (usually an older and successful business) and simply uses it as a template—making sure that every box is checked. The good news is that upon completion it is possible to publish an elegant organizational chart with all the supporting documentation. The bad news is that the org chart will have little if any correspondence with the emergent organization, and worse yet, it will introduce structures and functions that are not needed. Clearly this is the direct antithesis of the "minimal level of formal structure necessary to sustain the organization."

Perhaps it was an initial rush of enthusiasm, but when the phenomenon of self-organization was first discovered, the role of chaos received top billing. No doubt, chaos is important and very much present, but chaos is not the only thing. There is order too, as Dee Hock reminds us with his wonderful word, *Chaordic*. Life works itself out in an ancient dance between chaos and order. There are uncomfortable moments when chaos is the dominant mode, but there are equally periods of order, sometimes very long periods. And when those periods occur life becomes routine, fully equipped with standard procedures. An important part of formalizing the system is to record these procedures and make them available to newcomers. Equally important is the continuing awareness that the standard procedures are, like all other aspects of the formal system, only maps. Well done, these maps will enable the efficient prosecution of complex manufacturing processes along with all the other routines of organizational life, from Personnel to Finance. But at the end of the day, they are all still maps, subject to change as the system itself evolves and adapts. In short, the system drives the procedures, and not the other way around. And in no case will the procedures create the system, a clear example of getting the cart before the horse.

Required Organization

If the process of organizational formalization were entirely within the hands of the organization itself, adherence to the principle of "minimum level of necessary structure" would be relatively easy. However, the fact of the matter is that external forces require organizational structures which, in and of themselves, have little to do with the effective operation of the organization. For example, banks, shareholders, and government agencies demand certain structures and procedures. From their point of view, all of these "requirements" are useful and justified. But there does come a point where it may seem that the structure of your business is determined less by your own internal requirements than by the whims and dictates of outsiders.

Several possibilities present themselves by way of solution. If the required structure is little more than a formality, for example that a committee be established to meet once a year and certify the results of an election (or whatever), the obvious solution is create the committee, meet once a year, and do the required business in as little time as possible. However, when the required structural addition is more complex and/or of longer duration, some other strategy may be required.

Jonathan Shipyards (named for that dare-devil seagull) devised an interesting approach to a client's need for structure. Jonathan's major client was the U.S. Navy, and it was expected that all contractors would have a detailed organizational chart. The reason was simple, the Navy wanted to know who to call when issues arose with one of their ships. The problem for Jonathan was that the organizational structure of the company was essentially re-configured for each ship, and therefore any single organization chart would be fundamentally wrong in the majority of situations.

The solution was brilliant. Jonathan maintained an elaborate computer-based record of all related work for each ship—past, present, and future. And the opening screen of that computer record displayed the organization chart for that ship. The fact that some individual appeared as Project Director on this chart, and only as a minor functionary on some other, might confuse outsiders, but it made perfect sense to Jonathan. And besides, the people at Jonathan understood that the Navy, meaning the Captain of the Ship (or his contract officer), would in all likelihood, be only looking at one ship at a time—his ship. And when he took that look, he had all the information he expected or needed.

The Jonathan Solution may appear uncomfortably close to the questionable practice of maintaining two sets of books. But the problem with having two sets of books is less about having the two (or more) sets, than with how they are being used. If the intent is to hide nefarious activity from the eyes of those who have both the need and right to know, then the practice is not only questionable, it is criminal. However, if the intent is that of translation—translating actual practice into terms that can be accurately understood by an outsider or a newcomer, then we have a horse of a different color.

Accurate translation represents a core skill when it comes to providing useful maps of the territory for newcomers and outsiders. The key lies in understanding that different people, with different needs, require different maps. A tourist map, sufficient to get a visitor to an interesting restaurant will not work for a contractor seeking to avoid buried cables and water mains. And so also for banks, vendors, customers, and new employees. Each group will require its own special maps providing such information as is necessary for them to perform their functions.

Mapmaking for external groups is relatively simple and straightforward if for no other reason than that their needs are limited. As I mentioned, delivery trucks drivers need to know where the loading dock is located and the hours of operation. Simple well

placed signs are usually sufficient. The situation becomes much
more complicated when dealing with other groups, especially new
employees.

Enabling new employees to cross over the boundary and
become useful citizens is obviously a paramount concern, and creating an intuitive, well marked structure to guide them on their
way is essential. Some organizations seemingly adopt the principle
enunciated by the crusty old gentleman from Maine, who when
queried by a tourist about the lack of signs in his town replied—
"Well if you belonged here, you would know where you are." I suppose there is a certain Darwinian wisdom in all this, but it hardly
contributes to positive employee morale.

At the opposite end of the spectrum, other organizations simply bury the newcomers in a blizzard of information. Curiously
enough this approach has essentially the same disorienting effect as
the total lack of information. Finding an effective middle ground is
made considerably easier if the purpose of the structure is kept in
mind. There is no need to inform new employees about *everything*—
just those things necessary to get them started down the road.
Once on the road, they can and will find their way (or not), and
with a little luck they will shortly make the acquaintance of Lucy
and her colleagues.

Communication, Silos, and Circles

The lifeblood of all well-functioning self-organizing systems is
information regarding internal function and conditions in the environment. To the extent that this information is less than accurate
and free flowing, system function will decline. The reason is simple.

Without the essential information the adaptive process slows, or comes to a halt. And for a Complex *Adaptive* System—this is the end.

Ensuring the free flow of accurate information is the single most important concern under the heading of formalizing the system. It should be noted that this has nothing to do with organizing the system. Rather the intent is to enable the system to do for itself what only the system can do—provided effective means of communication are readily at hand.

Effective communication depends in the first instance upon the mental models of organization we hold, and the circle has obvious advantages. The elegant simplicity of communication in a circle radically contrasts with the byzantine pathways depicted by the common organizational chart. Even worse is the unofficial mental model of many organizations—silos. Hermetically sealed vertical columns, steadfastly protected from invading hordes—with minimal connections to other silos, but only at the top. I perversely imagine a narrow footbridge swaying in the wind, which is negotiated once a month by the VP in charge as he or she crosses over to the Senior Executive Committee meeting, located of course in that most isolated of all silos, the Executive Office Suite.

Not only is communication impeded by the silos, it is positively discouraged. Information passes, if at all, only to those with a certified need-to-know. The impenetrable silos supposedly have the advantage of keeping everything under control, and if they were truly successful, the organization would perish for lack of sustenance (information). Fortunately most silos are pretty leaky, and for sure the informal communication system goes into overdrive. But there is an unfortunate consequence. As the informal communication system

(Lucy and the watercooler) is repressed it goes underground and begins to reflect the conditions of its oppression. The message gets nasty and rumors fly. But people will communicate, and they do.

The usual justification for the silo approach to organization is the need for security, particularly in terms of proprietary information. There is no question that nasty people exist waiting to run off with the corporate jewels. That said, my friends in the security business tell me that the first, and best, defense for sensitive information is a dedicated people, who care about that information and understand its value. When people don't care and understand, real security is almost impossible. An even worse situation exists when the people are negatively disposed to the organization. No matter how high and protected the silos, they might as well be sieves.

Free, open communication which stimulates and informs the ongoing adaptive process is essential for the continued well–being of any self–organizing system. And the circle is an effective mental model of that system—a circle with nothing in the middle, nothing in the way so that all communication is straight line and direct. But how can we formalize the system in such a way as to support and sustain such a flowing state?

Twenty–five years ago the answer to that question came largely in terms of physical proximity. Formalizing the system to support communication usually meant creating physical structures which encouraged the free interchange of information. Concretely, this took the form of corporate campuses creating attractive co–locations for all members, and within the buildings "open office" configurations invited conversation. Add in what today seem like primitive electronics (phone, fax, telegraph, video), and the picture was complete. Physical proximity and the possibility of meeting face-to-face are still obviously important, but it now takes place in a totally new context. With the advent of the Internet and its various forms and functions (email, blogs, wikis, websites) we have entered a new reality.

In the new electronic environment the constraints of time and space are transformed and almost disappear. Everybody is equidistant from everybody else, and spatial and temporal location no longer count for all that much. It is all one big circle.

Not long ago, if you asked for somebody's address, you would be told something like "4th and Sycamore." Today the answer is very likely to be "hhowen@verizon.net." Perhaps even more curious, some "organizations" have no existence in time and space— they are "only" a website, a Dot Com. But strangest of all is how quickly this new reality has become commonplace.

The importance of the Internet to our present discussion of formalization of the system in support of rapid and effective communication should be obvious. We need it and it works. What may not be so obvious is the degree to which the Internet actually fosters the phenomenon of self-organization and, perhaps of equal importance, our own awareness of that phenomenon. In the early days, most people saw the Internet as a new communications tool, and therefore an extension, or refinement, of the tools they already had. Thus email took over from "snail mail." The truth, however, is rather deeper. The Internet is itself a self-organizing system.

Obviously some human beings have written programs and manufactured servers and desktops, but that is just the beginning. Once up and running, the Internet has taken on a life of its own.

Nobody controls it, although many have tried. Emergent organization is a daily phenomenon all without benefit of a CEO, Executive
Committee, or central planning body. It happens all by itself.

The self-organizing nature of the Internet is interesting in and
of itself, but more important for our immediate concern is that the
Internet is the natural, maybe even essential partner of that
self-organizing system known as your business or organization.
The Internet has the flexible capacity to follow and facilitate the
communication flow so essential to the well-being of the business.

When the Internet enters your organizational life, or even
becomes your organizational life, very practical needs for information
sharing are quickly taken care of in a most synergistic fashion. One
self-organizing system assisting another self-organizing system in
what may become a completely seamless and symbiotic manner.
And—there is a further benefit. The Internet can map your system
as you use it, and essentially in real time.

A major finding of the systems thinkers has been that a system
is its own best model (we might say map). Nothing else comes even
close. And if the business of formalizing the system is essentially a
matter of making good maps for visitors and newcomers, this
insight is very important. Of course there is also a difficulty. The
system, as its own map, is accurate to the last detail, but the very
complexity of all those details usually makes that map so turgidly
dense as to be unreadable. We are now back at square one. And we
would stay at square one were it not for a significant capacity of
the Internet: *It is searchable.*

For the customer seeking to rid himself of unwanted merchan-
dise, a few keystrokes can bring the needed information regarding

where, when, and how. Delivery trucks following the same approach can easily find the loading dock and hours of operation. Obviously all of this (and much more) is now common practice, and corporate giants such as Amazon.com have raised this practice to the level of high art. Many people would see this as simply good sense when it comes to customer and vendor service, which is undoubtedly true. But I would see it as superb mapmaking—the ultimate formalization of the system. You could think of this as the organizational equivalent of MapQuest.

For newcomers, seeking to make their way in the system and searching for Lucy, the electronic real time map is a godsend. It is doubtful that typing in "Lucy" would have positive results, but a search of ongoing projects could well produce a list of people and activities in alignment with the sorts of things a particular newcomer cared about. And, as we have seen, when there is a commonality of caring, bonds are formed, organization commences, and productive work gets done. No guarantees of course, save one: In the absence of caring, nothing much of utility takes place. And should the newcomer find nothing to care about, that person might save himself, and his new colleagues, a lot of pain and frustration were he to find an alternate place of employment. This is called exercising the Law of Two Feet.

The thought of having totally accurate and accessible maps of an organization is probably sufficient to drive the security conscious to distraction. And so it would be more than reasonable to have password protections to limit access, but note that there are delicate trade–offs. Extreme security will mean that the lifeblood of the self–organizing system is painfully restricted. It will also mean that the Informal (communication) System will go into hyperwarp

—for caring people will seek to do their job, even if they have to utilize back channels. The net effect will be that some considerable part of the truly creative work in the organization will be driven underground (skunkworks), take on a revolutionary flavor, and be largely unavailable to the organization as a whole as a source of inspiration and synergistic innovation. So the question becomes— How open can you be? The best answer may be something like—A little more open than you feel comfortable with, and less than some might desire.

With the advent of the Internet in the organizational world, the balance of power between the formal and the informal system seems ready to shift, indeed it may well have already shifted, to the consternation of those who hold the formal system preeminent. One might view the Internet as the ultimate watercooler (coffee station) and everybody is now invited into Lucy's Loop. Accepting that invitation is a matter of personal choice, but the access is now open. It would seem that not only have Lucy and the Informal System escaped from the closet, they are not far from taking over.

To be sure there are those who perceive (rightly) such open access as a genuine threat to formal system dominance and their own power and control. Accordingly they will make strong effort to restrict and constrain access, but that will be a difficult, perhaps impossible task. The sheer redundancy of the network makes closure a hard job, and as fast as one roadblock (net block) is set in place, the natural creativity of a self-organizing system finds a way around.

Of course, there is a solution to the difficulty—unplug the net. Very effective, but with an enormous cost. Close the net and virtually all information ceases to flow, at least all information useful for quick decisions in a fast changing world. A prime example of the moment is the People's Republic of China. Having made the decision to join the larger world in pursuit of economic development, they opened their borders physically and electronically. They now find themselves in a curious position. Their unprecedented economic growth in a global environment is sustainable only with full connections to that world, and internally amongst the multitude of their peoples—which their formal system finds distinctly uncomfortable. How all of this will end up is the trillion dollar question, but personally I would bet on Lucy and the money.

The Formal Leadership

Last, but by no means least, we come to the Formal Leadership. These individuals are the designated boundary keepers and official interfaces with the external world of vendors, service suppliers, and other interested parties, in addition to newcomers to the organization. The consideration of Formal Leadership here at the end is not to suggest that it is unimportant, however it is useful to understand the nature of organizational boundaries and the constituencies to be served before proceeding.

Creation of the Formal Leadership structure is best done in moderation, as is the case with all other aspects of formalizing the system. Unlike some contemporary organizations where it appears that absolutely everybody has a spot on the organization chart, usually with the title of vice president, leanness (but hopefully not meanness) will better serve the needs. The point is not to give everybody a title but rather to clearly indicate those people to whom outsiders and newcomers can turn for information and support—no more, no less.

When filling the roster, credibility counts. It is important that those who occupy the titled spots know what they are doing with a knowledge born of experience. This will mean that a prior demonstration of Authentic Leadership must be a fundamental criterion for selection. But it is even more important to remember what comes first. Titled positions do not confer, or guarantee, the power and prerogatives of leadership. All of that comes from the confluence of passion and responsibility which creates Authentic Leadership. The organization chart does not create leadership, even less—The Leader, but to be effective it will acknowledge the presence of real leadership. And should it occur that those holding the titled positions become little more than placeholders, some changes will be in order, lest the credibility of the total organization suffer.

Compensation

The organization chart historically has had a number of functions, one of which was to serve as the basis for the compensation schedule. It was presumed that those who occupied a higher position on the chart deserved higher levels of compensation, everybody on the same level deserved comparable compensation, and those not on the chart were relegated to the bottom of the heap. Leaders got more, workers got less, and you could tell who everybody was by their place on the chart, or absence from it.

There is an obvious logic and apparent fairness to this arrangement, provided the organizational form changed little over the years, and the details of job function could be defined precisely, allowing for predefined compensation packages and career ladders.

However, as we come to understand the nature and function of self–organizing systems, and more particularly, our businesses as self–organizing, the comforting logic and stability of the old organization chart, and related compensation schedule, fall into serious question.

In a situation where a particular person may simultaneously be a leader or worker in multiple different projects (jobs), all of which may change in an instant, providing adequate and fair compensation becomes a rather complex affair—too complex for the old arrangement. But what would constitute an appropriate alternative?

I confess that accounting and compensation management are not part of my skill base! But it occurs to me that the world of the independent consultant may provide some clues. For outsiders it may be more than difficult to see the consulting world as an organization, but as an insider, that is the way it has looked to me for better than 25 years. And it is totally self–organizing. Independent consultants have associations, networks, and common projects. At any given time they may be leader or worker, and often both at the same time. And The Leader has never been found. Confusing perhaps, but it makes sense to us—and we get paid. At least most of the time.

Whether this model would work more broadly I can't say. Which is only to underline the point I made at the start of *The Wave Rider's Guide to the Future*. This is not the final, definitive edition. But it is a start, and I believe you will find it to be an effective place to begin. Perhaps you will feel called upon to solve the riddle of compensation?

Chapter XVIII

A Day in the Life of . . .

S o what would it be like were you to take the plunge? Just imagine . . . It is a standard Monday morning in your place of business. Your inbox (electronic or wooden) is overflowing with requests, reports, along with small notes about possibly bright ideas, or eminently bad ones. And every piece of paper, or electronic notation, is only the leading edge of a web of complexity stretching outward in time and space, well beyond your capacity to see or sense.

Financial statements reflect the tremors of the rise and fall of currencies from a country you have never visited, whose culture you know only from newspaper snippets, and whose recent political currents disappear in a swirl of unknown issues and personalities. The announced resignation of a colleague sounds fairly straightforward, something about "pursuing new opportunities," but there is no information about why this is happening. Family breakdown, office politics, professional slight—all of the above, or none? A new technology is announced by a competitor which comes from a field of science with a name you can't even spell. That is just the top of the box—it just gets deeper, and this is just Monday morning. Your first cup of coffee is getting cold, and somehow you must make sense out of all this to the point that useful directions may be established, business be done, and not just any business but something approaching excellence, high performance. And to make things more interesting, it is not just any Monday morning, but your first Monday morning on the new job you had been hoping for. It isn't quite like being CEO, but you have your own Department—and now what?

Your first order of business might as well be a fresh cup of coffee. For certain you could use the caffeine, and the time away from that inbox will give you the opportunity to clear your head before your first staff meeting. And besides, you are on a mission: Find Lucy! Given her rank in the organization she will never show up for the staff gathering, and even if she did, she probably wouldn't say much, but with a little luck you may just run into her in her native domain. Don't count on Lucy to be wearing a sign around her neck, but as you watch the ebb and flow of folks around the coffeepot, pay close attention to that special person everybody just seems to know. That could be Lucy, or a similar person with a different name. Since you are a newcomer, an unknown quantity, don't expect an immediate welcome, even less that you will be privileged with all the latest information, but keep at it. Lucy is out there somewhere and you need her every bit as much as she needs you.

Now for that staff meeting. Feeling somewhat guilty because you have no carefully prepared agenda, which as everybody knows is absolutely essential for a productive meeting, you dive right in. Greeting your new staff, most of whom you know only by name, you invite each one to identify those hot issues for the Department that they feel a special passion for, write them down on a piece of paper, and post it on the wall. After a moment of shock, they oblige, and soon the wall is covered with papers. It definitely looks chaotic, but if you wanted to know what was on the Departmental mind—it was all on the wall, and it took about 10 minutes. Then you asked everybody to sign up for any issue they would like to pursue, and with a little negotiation for time and space, small discussion groups form all over the room.

As you look over the posted issues, it occurs to you that every issue you had thought might be important was on the wall—along with a whole mess more that you never considered. For the next hour or so, the discussion was hot and heavy, and there was really nothing for you to do but wander from group to group, making what small contributions you could, and most of all, listening.

When the decibel level dropped, you asked the leaders of each group to quickly summarize where they had been, next steps, what they needed to go forward, and it was time for lunch. Amazing—in a little over two hours the system had virtually mapped itself. Not completely, and for sure you didn't understand it all, but for a first cut, it wasn't bad. In addition to the identification of hot issues, you had a great introduction to the natural flow of the group, and even more interesting, the personalities and interactions of the people involved. There were some surprises. People, who on first meeting you took to be retiring and noncontributory, showed themselves to be firestorms of activity and contribution. Authentic Leadership, perhaps? And a few of the supposed "superstars" seemed something less than supernovas. Could have been just an off day—or something more?

And you did virtually nothing! No prepared agenda, no tense moments corralling discussion, shepherding egos, and defending your authority. You just walked around and listened, and everything just happened all by itself. Could this be what wave riding is all about? Probably not, but at least you know where the water is, and with a little practice it could get better.

Lunch, and a moment for a deep breath, interrupted almost immediately by the gentle vibration of the pager on your belt. Call your office! You take another cup of coffee and head back. There are two messages. The first from corporate staff saying that a major "new product" project for your department has been approved— with a scorchingly high priority. Needs to be done Now! The second message, and a most disturbing one, comes from the manager of a neighboring department, saying in no uncertain terms that while he is totally in favor of the project, he is absolutely opposed to the idea that your department will be given the lead. Sounds like chaos, confusion, and conflict in abundance. And this is just your first day.

A few of your staff are still in the conference room finishing up the morning's work. You share the messages and ask their opinion. The first reaction is an odd combination of jubilation and shock. They are delighted that the project has come through because they had all worked long and hard on the development. They are dismayed by the other manager's opposition, made all the more painful because support and cooperation from that department will be essential for the project's success. What to do?

Some of your old-timers advocate a straight power play from the top. After all Corporate has been clear in its directions and assignment of responsibility. Now would be a very good time to see if they are serious. A word from the CEO should put the opposition in its place. But the downside is obvious. A power play could squelch the opposition, but the needed support and cooperation would likely evaporate as well, leading to the project's failure. Seems like your river is running rapidly with all sorts of whirlpools and standing waves.

There is another option: Open some space and see if the swirling currents of chaos, conflict, and confusion can find some new and higher order of complexity—provided they had the space to engage each other in a useful fashion. Actually that seems like the only option because the end result of the power play would doubtless be a pyrrhic victory. Turf protected. Project failed.

The clock is ticking, but opening space requires little preparation—just a place to meet and the people who care. Fortunately the large conference room is available, and you send out an invitation to everybody you can think of who might care about the project. Time: 9:00 am tomorrow. Theme: "Creating a Successful Project." No mention of the turf battle, but there is no need because everybody already knows. And besides, concentrating on that conflict would only intensify it. Some of your staff are saying that with such a short lead time they wonder if anybody will come. And of course you don't know. But it is amazing how quickly schedules are cleared if the priority is high enough. And this is a biggie, not only for you but for the whole company. At least that is what Corporate has said.

Morning comes and by 9 o'clock the room is full. Not just the usual suspects (your department and the opposition) but all sorts of other people who for their own reasons care about the project. As things get under way, people leave their seats in the circle to announce the particular issues they care about relative to making the project a success. The famous Turf Battle is one of the issues raised, but it is quickly overwhelmed by a torrent of others dealing with technical development, marketing, resources, and future actions. Groups form and discussions flow during the day. Surprisingly the tense confrontation of the early morning gives way to something approaching excitement as people discuss new ideas, approaches, and areas of collaboration. It becomes apparent that they have much more in common than they do in difference, although differences certainly remain. However, the stark face-off between you and your opposite number has now been bounded and outflanked by the energy and enthusiasm of the assembled group. Power play has given way to power flow—all to the benefit of the new project.

As the day comes to a close it is clear that everything isn't pretty and hardly perfect. In fact there is an enormous amount of work to be done. It is also clear that the people and the energy are in place to move the job. What is remarkable is that you didn't do it, and more to the point you couldn't if you had wanted to. The pieces were too complex, the forces too powerful. Nevertheless, your presence was very important, but not for purposes of command and control. All you did was to invite anybody who cared to join together in the creation of the new project and then opened some space.

In the following days the new project came to life, but in ways that differed radically from traditional expectations. Most striking was the fact that the project was no longer "your project," or even your department's project—it was now clearly owned by all those who cared. And this caring community was quite remarkable for its diversity. Not only did it cross departmental lines, including that infamous department which had shown every sign of being your mortal nemesis, but outsiders as well, including potential customers.

When the customers had shown up at the original gathering, more than a few questioning eyebrows were raised. After all, things could get out of control in terms of such sticky issues as proprietary secrets. And of course similar concerns existed relative to the other departments in your own organization. What could possibly prevent somebody from running off with the bacon and stealing the whole show? Obviously the stakes were high, and if you thought about it too much, it could be very nervous making to be sure. Those concerns certainly represent one side of the coin, but the flip side showed a very different face.

On the other side of the coin, the level of creative interaction that emerged from the initial gathering was truly awesome. Groups which had formed around issues of common concern continued to meet face-to-face, or electronically, as they pushed their concerns toward meaningful resolution. Some met often, others hardly at all, and a few never got together, having either come to some useful conclusion, or deciding that the issue they had identified was not worthy of further pursuit. Attempting to follow this maelstrom of effort would have been quite impossible save for the existence of the dedicated website which had been created before the first gathering. As each group did its work, reports of current activities and future efforts were posted. All interested parties could search that increasing mass of complex information to see what was going on, make suggestions, offer assistance—and when needed, create new nodal points of action (Nexi of Caring). The project had become a living thing constantly adapting to emerging opportunities and challenges, all taking place at mind–numbing speed.

Exciting for sure, and not without some interesting transformations. As the people engaged their work, ideas and proposals shot back and forth, most of which showed up online, but the coffee station was often the site of heated debate. In a strange and wonderful way the informal communications system had become a powerful and positive ally. No longer the nefarious nest of insidious gossip, it became a critical meeting point where new ideas could be vetted, and new alliances formed.

There were also more than a few white knuckle moments. As people engaged and passions rose, conflict was an inevitable companion. At times it seemed that the opposing parties would tear each other apart to the ultimate detriment of the project. But just when it seemed that disaster was inescapable, you remembered the critical mantra, Keep the Space Open.

In other days and times you would have thought it to be your special duty to dampen the passion and resolve the conflict—but it was now very clear that the passion was the essential engine for the project's success. At the same time you were profoundly, and humbly, aware that the complex intertwining interests and ideas were well beyond your capacity to understand and sort them out. And even if you had the necessary experience and capacity, it remained true that only the conflicted parties themselves held the key. Only they really knew the details, and they were the ones who were going to have to work together—or not. Solution? Open some space and invite those who cared to find the way forward.

A case in point began quietly enough. One of the working groups, which had undertaken the task of refining the product design to most neatly meet market needs and expectations, suddenly found itself at a crossroads. Part of the group favored one design and the balance of the group favored another. Emails flew, small groups gathered at the coffee station, and it looked for a time that the growing conflict could derail the whole project. Just about then appeals from the several parties began showing up in your electronic in-basket, suggesting that you use your authority, as department head, and make a decision.

In fact you had the authority, and to be honest you also had your favorite solution. Making the choice would be no big deal, at least on paper. It was also quite likely that your decision would remain a "paper decision," or worse—that there would be some unintended consequences. The reality of the situation created some costs and opportunities that must be carefully considered. On the cost side, you recognized that this work group (like all the working groups) consisted of individuals from all over the company as well as customers, who had chosen to devote their time, energy, and expertise because they cared to do so. Were you to preemptively eliminate the object of their caring, the chances were better than even that they would quickly find better things to do. That in itself might be an acceptable cost, but in all fairness you also had to admit that both designs had merit.

With these thoughts in mind, you decided to spend a little time at the coffee station where the contending parties could often be found. When the opportunity presented itself you casually mentioned that perhaps there were actually two designs and two markets. Instead of going for One Right Way—go for both and see what happened.

It took very little time for the informal communication system to percolate through and do its work, and the next you heard about the situation was that the group had decided to divide (creative use of the Law of Two Feet) and pursue both designs. Some of your fellow department heads grumbled about gross inefficiency and lack of executive decisiveness, but you felt that two products for two marketplaces could well end up being a marvelous double win. Time would tell.

As days became weeks, and the time for roll-out neared, the working groups naturally focused and brought their discussions down to the fine details necessary for implementation. To be sure you had indicated a hoped for time frame at the beginning which would fit with the corporate life cycle and the natural cycles of your intended markets. But never did you use your authority to enforce the time lines, and truthfully there was no need, for the people involved seemed absolutely driven to bring *their* product to market. Never in your wildest dreams could you imagine asking anybody to devote the energy and hours to the enterprise which the group as a whole contributed. In the first place it would have been illegal in terms of their contracts, and besides, most of the people involved didn't "work" for you anyhow. Truthfully, you often found yourself begging the people to take a break. So much for the hard driving executive!

As for the "duplicate designs"—that turned out to be a real winner. One of the designs (your favorite as it happened) fit most naturally with current opportunities and resources. But the second was scarcely a loss. That design and the people who cared for it simply spun off. For a little while it seemed that they had disappeared, and lacking official budget and sanction they found themselves to be in the status of an emerging skunkworks. However, as their plans came together the needed resources seemed to appear as if by magic, liberated, as it were. One fine day everything emerged Post-it like, to claim a place in the company product line. The Planning Department was of course unhappy, but everybody else simply enjoyed the substantial addition to the bottom line.

So was it just a fairy tale? Maybe—at least until you make it your own tale. It is also true that it all happened, though not necessarily in the sequence given. For another tale that definitely happened and told by a true Wave Rider, read on. Dee Hock, CEO *Emeritus* of VISA International, tells this story from his own experience.

Dee Hock: Wave Rider

VISA International is the largest business organization in the world with a turnover 10 times that of Wal–Mart and a market value of twice that of General Electric, according to Peter Senge in the Foreword of *One from Many*, Dee Hock's remarkable book.[23] Apart from its sheer size, what makes it significant, particularly for our concerns, is the manner in which it grew and continues to exist. Unlike virtually all similar corporate ventures there was no single, all powerful CEO, nor a carefully designed strategic plan and organizational structure. Rigid command and control mechanisms were

---

23 Dee Hock, *One from Many: VISA and the Rise of Chaordic Organization* (Berrett-Koehler, 2005, p. ix).

most evident by their absence. VISA International grew as a self–organizing system, a child of nature, a rain forest, according to Dee Hock. In the following story Hock describes an early adventure on the way to the birthing of VISA. I know you will feel the passion of the moment, and I think you can perceive the *modus operandi* of a skillful Wave Rider.

At the time of Hock's story, VISA International was not even a possibility, and the scene is set in the bank where Hock and his colleagues struggled to join the raging mania of the Credit Card Business. Nobody had ever done that business before, and although there were plans and procedures, along with rudimentary equipment, putting it all together was a totally new adventure. As we all know, plans often fall apart the moment they move from the ideal, stable world of the printed page into the vortex of everyday living. The immediate task was mailing 100,000 credit cards to their new owners, and it was headed straight for disaster. Hock writes—

Something is sadly awry. The form–feeder cannot be synchronized with the printer. Both machines constantly jam. As mailers flow erratically from the printer, cutting and folding machinery slices some in half and crumples others. Technicians are bent over, heads and hands deep in the machinery. The supplier soon confesses. The whole setup is untested. They've never used it before, and it's an abysmal failure.

Bob and I walk away to a quiet corner near a supply closet to console one another. There is no possibility of another block of time on the computer. Without mailers by morning, the whole thing is off. How can we explain our failure to Maxwell Carlson, a hundred thousand customers waiting for their promised cards, and hundreds of merchants waiting for those customers? Our minds are racing in a hundred directions seeking a way out. Bob is leaning on the handle of a push broom.

Inspiration is often the child of desperation. Could he be leaning on the answer? We quickly unscrew the handle, rush to the stack of mailers and shove it through a roll. With a heave we lift it—might even be able to hold it for half an hour at a stretch, maybe more—or prop it up on cabinets. The broom handle makes a decent axle. With a third person to guide forms into the computer and enough three-person crews, it might work. Other crews could wind mailers on broom handles as they came from the printer. With enough crews we might get mailers printed. We can worry about cutting and folding another day.

We call everyone in the area together, printing company executives, bank officers, programmers, operators, janitors —everyone. There is no need for blame. Will they work the night—no bosses—no procedures—just grab a piece of the problem and get it done? Need help, ask—want to help, offer. Yes? Good! Two people lift a roll of mailers and the printer begins to chatter. Two others grab a second broom handle and begin to roll up mailers as they emerge. Ideas pour out from everyone and someone is instantly on the way to attend to each. "Search the building and steal broom handles, Get food and drinks sent in." "We'll need gloves." "Round up relief crews." "Rig a backup printer." No one knows all that is happening and no one has time to care. We must trust. The last roll comes off the printer at six in the morning. An exhausted, happy band of brothers and sisters head home to catch a few hours of sleep before the next ordeal begins. As we labored through the night, someone had not only claimed ownership of every aspect of the night's work, but future work separating and folding mailers to get the project back on track. Is that how the future happens? Ingenuity? Passion? Spontaneous order out of chaos? It seems so, as long as control is kept on a leash.[24]

I would be delighted were I able to report that Dee Hock had read my suggestions for operating in a self-organizing environment. But this adventure took place in 1966 at a time when I was doing community organization in the streets of Washington, DC, and Open Space Technology had yet to emerge from the bottom of a martini glass. That said, I believe you can easily see the steps of a very competent Wave Rider, heading towards High Performance. Hock clearly did his homework and made a plan, as well as he was able. That homework created a map which got him to the head of the trail—but once the trail was engaged, it became much more rugged and challenging than the map had indicated. Surprise!

When disaster struck and the mailers were being sliced, diced, and spread on the floor, Hock could have spread blame over every likely candidate, beginning with the technicians. As the senior executive present, he could have loudly asserted his right for

---

24 *Op. cit.* p. 70.

control, and done everything in his power to render order out of chaos, and return to The Plan. But he didn't. Instead he simply opened space (small "o" and small "s") and invited (clearly did not "command") everyone who cared, or might care, to bring their whole selves (passion and responsibility) to the task. While they obviously didn't sit in a circle, the rigid hierarchy of the old Organization Chart was nowhere to be found, and were you to draw a picture of the emergent organization, a circle of peers and colleagues would not be far from the mark. However, drawing any sort of a picture would be difficult, if only because of the high velocity, kinetic action of the group. Talk about *Law of Two Feet*—it was constantly observed.

As for the Four Principles, they were all clearly in operation. No one worried that the "right" people were not on hand, for the right people were obviously present—the ones who cared. And for sure nobody had time to cry over what could have been, or might have been as they concentrated on that present moment, knowing (if not saying), "Whatever happens is the only thing that could have." There was no time line or timetable, and if there was it had no effect—"Whenever it starts is the right time" and not a moment too soon. When it was over, it was over—the mailers were ready for delivery and perhaps most significantly, "An exhausted, *happy* (italics mine) band of brothers and sisters head home to catch a few hours of sleep." The important word is "happy." This was real High Performance as measured by the fact that an impossible task was accomplished in unbelievable time *and* those who did it all actually enjoyed what they were doing. My words for it are High Play. And please note: The Leader was nowhere in sight.

Conclusion

This is a conclusion only in the sense that it represents the end of the book. In fact we are dealing with a work in progress. In the beginning I described the undertaking as an ongoing experiment which for me has been running for more than twenty years. Based on that experience I offered certain propositions about the nature of our world and our organizations, combined with an approach to effective navigation (Wave Riding). I am under no illusions that anything close to ironclad proof has been achieved. Nor would I ask that you simply believe what I have said. Indeed, quite the opposite. It is my fervent hope that you will believe nothing until it is validated in your own experience. In short, please run the experiment for yourself. I am hopeful that your findings will parallel my own, but where they differ we will have a marvelous opportunity for deeper learning.

The fundamental proposition is simply stated: *There is no such thing as a non–self-organizing system.* All systems, from the total cosmos down to the smallest collection of quarks, are the product of the elegantly simple process of self-organization. Not just a little bit, or in some distant corner, but everywhere and in every time—it is turtles all the way down.

Human systems are no exception. A small mom and pop store, a major corporation, or an entire country, all are self-organizing,

231

despite what we may have been taught and practiced. Here is a major turn in the road requiring a massive shift in thinking. We have been taught that human systems/organizations came into existence by dint of our effort. We organized them and we are, or should be, in charge. If the stated proposition is sound we face a very different world.

Making the required shift in thinking is perhaps as radical in its own sphere as the move from Newtonian physics to quantum mechanics, and for many of the same reasons. As the community of physicists ventured ever deeper into the subatomic world, they discovered a strange new world indeed. Space bent, time seemingly could go backward, and the rock solid certainty and order of Newton's vision dissolved in indeterminacy. The emerging theory seemed crazy to many, including those who propounded it. And the oddness of the situation was only compounded by the fact that in certain situations, Newton's theory still worked. The lever still operated as Newton predicted it would, and our successful efforts to fly to the moon were based on classic Newtonian physics.

Now more than 100 years from the first emergence of the quantum revolution, it is still true; Newton works. But there is a difference, Newtonian thinking is now contexted by quantum theory. This means that for simple and very practical things, Newton will do. However, if one is searching for a deeper, more elegant understanding there is no choice but to enter the quantum world. Once in that world, we encountered, and have learned to use, a power so massive that it dwarfs anything that Newton could imagine. The fruits of our endeavor are visible everywhere—for better or for worse. From the hydrogen bomb to modern medical imagery

(MRI)—all have emerged from the strange quantum world. And it is also true; Newton still works.

The proposed shift in thinking brings us to a point where everything is seen to be self-organizing, even and perhaps most especially, all those things we thought we organized and must control. This can be a very hard pill to swallow, for it suggests that much of what we have spent a great deal of time and effort working on (organizing things) was wasted. And to the extent that control, and the exercise of control, is critical to our own sense of self-worth, that prop to our ego is knocked down. It turns out that we were never in control and never could be, at least in any absolute sense. However, what may be bad news for the ego turns out to be good news for our stressed and overworked selves. We have been relieved of a massive task made even worse by the fact that we never quite reached the goal, at least according to The Plan.

As with the case of Newton, our old understandings and approaches still seem to work, at least in limited situations. We may therefore choose to avoid the shift and continue our belief that we are the organizers with the right of control. But there is a major cost. We find our understanding of how things are supposed to work challenged by odd anomalies—things just don't work as they were supposed to. And our efforts to organize and control stress us out, often leaving us like Sisyphus watching the rock of unintended consequences and failing endeavors roll back upon us. But we do have a choice.

When we make the choice to see self-organization as fundamental to our world, our condition improves immeasurably. To begin with, many troublesome, anomalous, and counterintuitive experiences now make sense. In fact they are even predictable. No longer do we have to overlook, or explain away, these aberrancies in order to maintain our ordered sense of the world. And our tasks in this world, such as making a living and doing business, may now be accomplished in a most economic fashion with optimal results. We can effectively collaborate with the fundamental power of self-organization to achieve what could never be achieved by our strength and wisdom alone. In a word, we become conscious and skillful Wave Riders.

Of course we have always been Wave Riders, if only intuitively, and all too often with a sense of guilt. We live in a self-organizing world, even if we didn't know it, and we have practiced the art of Wave Riding, albeit in secret. Each time we participated in the Informal Communications System and furtively talked to Lucy, we entered the world of self-organizing systems, but usually with some sense of guilt because we weren't playing by the rules. But that secretive stance need not continue, for Lucy and the Informal System have come out of the closet, and it is time to acknowledge Lucy as one of our friends.

Since we have always been Wave Riders, the required shift in thinking and change in behavior is not as radical as it may sound. We need only to do consciously and intentionally what we have been doing ever since. It is a case of fully becoming what we already are. The steps along the way are outlined in *The Wave Rider's Guide*, and I believe you will find them more than sufficient to bring you to the edge of the water and give you a start on your first ride. After that, it is pretty much up to you.

And just a word of advice. As you start your practice of Wave Riding, do not attempt to ride a championship wave your first time out, a Maverick for example. Start with the small ones, which might mean using Open Space Technology for a staff meeting, building a team by invitation as opposed to assignment, or simply sit in a circle. Over time you will find your footing, and the time will come when the challenge of a Maverick will be welcomed.

Index

About the Author

Harrison Owen is president of H. H. Owen and Company. His academic background and training centered on the nature and function of myth, ritual, and culture. In the mid-1960s, he left academe to work with a variety of organizations, including small West African villages, urban community organizations (both in the United States and in Africa), the Peace Corps, regional medical programs, the U.S. National Institutes of Health, and the U.S. Veterans Administration. Along the way, he discovered that his study of myth, ritual, and culture had direct application to these social systems. In 1977, he created H. H. Owen and Company in order to explore the culture of organizations in transformation as a theorist and practicing consultant. Harrison convened the First International Symposium on Organization Transformation and is the originator of Open Space Technology. He is the author of *Open Space Technology: The Users Guide; Spirit: Transformation and Development in Organization; Leadership Is; Riding the Tiger; The Millennium Organization; Tales from Open Space; and Expanding Our Now: The Story of Open Space Technology.*

Some of Harrison Owen's client engagements and presentations include: Owens/Corning Fiberglas, Procter and Gamble, Dupont,

Eastern Virginia Medical Authority, Shell/Netherlands, Shell Tankers (Dutch), Shell/Canada, the French Ministry of Telecommunications (PTT), the U.S. Forest Service, the U.S. Internal Revenue Service, Jonathan Corporation, the U.S. Army, Ikea (Sweden), Statoil (Norway), SAS Airlines, Young Presidents Organization, City University Business School (London), Gronigen University Business School (Holland), Taj Hotel Group (India), Congresso de Desarrollo Organizacional (Mexico), PepsiCola (Venezuela), National Education Association, Toronto–Dominion Bank (Canada), American Management Systems, American Society of Training and Development, Scott Paper, TEL–CEL/Venezuela, the American Society of Association Executives, the Presbyterian Church (USA), the Accor Hotel Group (France), Ermetek Corp (South Africa), the Union of International Associations (Belgium), Rockport Shoes, Corporate Express, the World Bank, AT&T, IBM, USWEST, the Organization Development Network, Lucent Technologies, and the Bank of Montreal.

About Berrett-Koehler Publishers

Berrett-Koehler is an independent publisher dedicated to an ambitious mission: Creating a World that Works for All.

We believe that to truly create a better world, action is needed at all levels—individual, organizational, and societal. At the individual level, our publications help people align their lives with their values and with their aspirations for a better world. At the organizational level, our publications promote progressive leadership and management practices, socially responsible approaches to business, and humane and effective organizations. At the societal level, our publications advance social and economic justice, shared prosperity, sustainability, and new solutions to national and global issues.

A major theme of our publications is "Opening Up New Space." They challenge conventional thinking, introduce new ideas, and foster positive change. Their common quest is changing the underlying beliefs, mindsets, institutions, and structures that keep generating the same cycles of problems, no matter who our leaders are or what improvement programs we adopt.

We strive to practice what we preach–to operate our publishing company in line with the ideas in our books. At the core of our approach is *stewardship*, which we define as a deep sense of responsibility to administer the company for the benefit of all of our "stakeholder" groups: authors, customers, employees, investors, service providers, and the communities and environment around us.

We are grateful to the thousands of readers, authors, and other friends of the company who consider themselves to be part of the "BK Community." We hope that you, too, will join us in our mission.

Be Connected

Visit Our Website

Go to www.bkconnection.com to read exclusive previews and excerpts of new books, find detailed information on all Berrett-Koehler titles and authors, browse subject-area libraries of books, and get special discounts.

Subscribe to Our Free E-Newsletter

Be the first to hear about new publications, special discount offers, exclusive articles, news about bestsellers, and more! Get on the list for our free e-newsletter by going to www.bkconnection.com.

Get Quantity Discounts

Berrett-Koehler books are available at quantity discounts for orders of ten or more copies. Please call us toll-free at (800) 929-2929 or email us at bkp.orders@aidcvt.com.

Host a Reading Group

For tips on how to form and carry on a book reading group in your workplace or community, see our website at *www.bkconnection.com.*

Join the BK Community

Thousands of readers of our books have become part of the "BK Community" by participating in events featuring our authors, reviewing draft manuscripts of forthcoming books, spreading the word about their favorite books, and supporting our publishing program in other ways. If you would like to join the BK Community, please contact us at bkcommunity@bkpub.com.